RUN
WITH ME

THE STORY OF A U.S. OLYMPIC CHAMPION

RUN
WITH ME

THE STORY OF A U.S.
OLYMPIC CHAMPION

SANYA
RICHARDS-ROSS

ZONDERKIDZ

Run with Me
Copyright © 2017 by Sanya Richards-Ross

This title is also available as a Zondervan ebook.

Requests for information should be addressed to:
Zondervan, *3900 Sparks Dr. SE, Grand Rapids, Michigan 49546*

ISBN 978-0-310-76121-1

All photos courtesy of the author unless otherwise noted.
Interior design: Denise Froehlich

Printed in the United States of America

17 18 19 20 21 22 23 24 25 /LSC/ 15 14 13 12 11 10 9 8 7 6 5 4 3 2 1

CONTENTS

The 4 Ps—Push, Pace, Position, Poise

PUSH—Chasing Your Dream

PACE—Finding Rhythm with God

POSITION—Finally Ready to Race

POISE—Commit to the Finish

My Future Children,

I haven't given birth to you yet, but I already love you so much. My prayer is to be half the parents my mom and dad were to me, by loving you and supporting your dreams in every way I can. I hope that one day you'll read *Run With Me* and feel like it's an honest guide to how I achieved success on the track, became the person I am today, and how you can achieve success in anything you choose.

To my future, to you . . . I love you!

Sanya Richards-Ross, Mom.

INTRODUCTION

When I first started running track, I never thought I'd run the 400-meter sprint. I loved the shorter races.

The 100-meters is an all-out sprint. You explode out of the starting block and power your way down the track. After about ten seconds of giving everything you have, the race is over. The 200-meters requires a bit more technique. This race is often decided by who can run the curve the best. The 100m goes in a straight line, while the 200m runs halfway around the track.

Then there's the 400-meters—one full lap. Track experts say it's the toughest race, the ultimate sprint. To be the world's best, you must have a good start, solid running form, a well-thought-out strategy, and a strong mind. The 400m is truly a battle between mind and body. After the first 300 meters, everything in your mind begs your body to stop. Just stop the pain of running that fast for that long. But the body must keep pushing.

It's pushing through that mental and physical pain that keeps a lot of runners away from the quarter mile.

I've always said I didn't choose the quarter mile. It chose me. Over time, I learned to love the race. My favorite part became the last 100 meters off the final curve. I felt free, like I was flying down the home stretch.

The track has always been my safe haven—my sanctuary, my place of peace. This is where I've always felt the most free.

But then, in a heartbeat, that freedom can turn to panic.

At the end of the 400-meters, you can sense the other athletes charging around you. Instead of feeling free, you can start to fear you're not in position to win. Your solid prerace strategy can be overtaken by an intense desire for victory. If you have to hurl your body across the finish line, you'll do it. You'll do whatever it takes to win. It's an instinct that comes over you as you sprint the final few meters.

Then, after making it through the tape, you have to wait. Heart pounding, body shaking, you wait in faith.

When I won the Olympic gold medal at the 2012 London Olympics, I wasn't 100 percent sure I had crossed the line first. It took a few seconds between the end of the race and hearing my name announced as the winner. During the wait I wanted desperately for my name to be at the top of the scoreboard. But I could only clasp my hands in prayer and trust God for the outcome.

The photo finish showed I had won comfortably, by a stride's length. But in the race's final moments, I dipped my left shoulder and stretched my neck out over the line. Even to this day, when I see my right arm punching through the air, I don't know if it's in celebration or a last-second reach to grab victory.

A True Champion

For as long as I can remember, my life has been measured in seconds. The fewer, the better. Most people equate success with having more. My quest was always for less. I've run and competed in track since I was seven years old.

When I first stepped on the track at Vaz Prep to represent my elementary school in Jamaica, I heard my parents, family, classmates, and friends cheering for me.

"Sanya a champion! Sanya a champion!" everyone called out. I would beat the other runners by a wide margin. The next day in our local newspaper, *The Gleaner*, my name was in the headlines.

I felt special. I was a champion. For more than two decades, I ran in circles around the track chasing that same feeling—the feeling of being a champion. My goal was to run a 400-meter race in 50 seconds, hopefully 49 or, even better, 48. My greatest source of validation was crossing the finish line first.

It took some time for me to realize I was of more value than a gold medal or a record-setting lap around the track. For so long, I was just Sanya Richards, the athlete. I hung my head when I didn't run well. My existence was all about my performance. Each loss came with a feeling of unhealthy and unwanted shame.

That's a trap many of us fall into. But God doesn't look at our athletic performance. He cares about our faithfulness. Running is just what I do. It's not who I am.

I am a child of God on a mission to use my talents to the best of my ability. To this day I'm still on a quest for less—less of me and more of God. I want to grow to become the best version of myself and help others do the same. Running is my platform. It's my foundation. God created me to run. By running, I give that gift back to him.

My faith, my walk with Christ, intensifies when I'm on the track. On that warm August night in London, I lunged my body forward, unsure of where it would land. I only had my faith.

Sometimes, we need moments like that. We need times when we are forced to be still, rely on our faith, and wait for the photo finish.

In many ways, life is nothing more than a collection of photo finishes, shot through the lens of God's camera. For every exciting high like the one I experienced in 2012, there have been just as many—if not more—excruciating lows.

After some especially difficult setbacks, I couldn't understand how I lost after I had trained so hard and competed with such focus. Eventually, I began to see that the losses were as significant as the wins.

That's the beauty of God's timing. We may not always understand why things happen, but if we wait on the Lord, we'll often see his plan. The Bible tells us: "Those who hope in the Lord will renew their strength. They will soar on wings like eagles; they will run and not grow weary, they will walk and not be faint." We can always trust him.

The lessons I learned didn't just make me a better runner. They molded me into a stronger person. Through this book, I hope my stories will help you see your own experiences through God's lens. No matter where your talents lie, you can use them to glorify God.

My journey carried me beyond the track. God has an amazing journey waiting for you, as well, as you follow him.

Now I look forward to my future and trust his planning. My hope is that you will do the same. God wants you to finish your race, whatever race it is, with grace. He gave me a strategy to do that—one that I want to share with you.

Just like the 400-meters requires a solid strategy, so does life. The four Ps—Push, Pace, Position, and Poise—made me a champion on the track. By following them (and a fifth "secret" P), we can all live an abundant life and cross the finish line with our heads held high, knowing we ran our best race.

The Four Ps—Push, Pace, Position, Poise

Years ago, when I started training with Coach Clyde Hart, he divided the 400-meter race into four phases. Coach Hart called them the 4 Ps—Push, Pace, Position, and Poise.

I worked on each of the four phases in every practice. Then when it came time to race, my body responded as my mind instinctively shifted from one phase to the next.

As I've gotten older, I still see the wisdom in Coach Hart's strategy. In some ways, even when I'm not on the track, I'm either pushing, pacing, positioning, or remaining poised and prayerful (*prayer* is the "secret" fifth P).

I hope you, too, can apply this strategy. By learning how to run your best race, you'll also learn how to live your best life.

Push—Chase Your Dream

The *push* part of the race takes intense focus and commitment.

You begin by setting your feet in the starting block, crouching over the track, and placing your fingertips just behind the line. As the starter raises his pistol, lift your hips into the set position and brace your body on your fingers. At the same time, prepare your mind to go from resting to full speed in a matter of seconds.

Bang!

The gun goes off. You explode from the blocks, going from

zero to twenty miles per hour in just a few strides. You push through the first part of the race with all your might. The start is a power event. The force from your feet pounding into the track allows the track to launch you forward into the next step. With the technology of today's tracks, the more you push into them, the more you get in return.

Life also gives back what you put into it. Every day, you have the opportunity to push yourself into a higher gear or achieve a goal. Whether it's taking honors courses in school, making time to exercise, or devoting extra focus to a special talent, you should propel forward on a mission.

Believe that your efforts will be rewarded. You may not be able to see it, or immediately feel it, but life honors hard work.

Pace—Create Your Rhythm

After getting out of the blocks strong, the first 100 meters of the race are run at nearly maximum speed. It's not possible, however, to maintain that pace throughout the entire quarter-mile. The human body cannot push that hard for that long.

At 100 meters, you have to throttle back and let your energy supplies refill with a little more oxygen. Your stride stretches out as your body finds a smooth tempo. Arms and legs work together with the lungs to sustain the energy and strength necessary to shift to another gear and kick down the home stretch.

Just like runners need to find a rhythm they can settle into, everyone needs an awareness of what they can handle. The *push* phase sets you up to chase down your dreams, but *pacing* allows you to maintain and keep going for the long haul. Rhythm and routine set you up for greatness.

Evaluate what your mind and body can maintain, what you can handle. Make sure your priorities don't cause your spirit to burn out. Check in with your Creator so that your vision aligns with his purpose for you. Keep your pace in line with God's. Running ahead of him may get you in trouble.

Position—Go with Courage

When you're racing the 400, you don't start to really compete until the 200-meter mark. As you begin to work the final turn, you consider where your competition is and how the race will be won.

You prepare the body to throttle back to full speed. It's a snap-quick decision.

Decide. Then, go for it.

It takes courage to execute the race plan. Coach Hart always said, "Most people will relax into the curve, but this is your advantage. This is where you have to start your kick. If you don't start your work here, you will lose seconds, and you won't be able to make them up."

Taking your position requires faith, discipline, and determination.

Where am I going? How badly do I want it? Will I stick to my plan when faced with struggle, pain, fear, and doubt?

Evaluate all these factors as you decide what you want out of life, what you want from your personal race, and what is required to get there.

Poise—Commit to the Finish

The final 100 meters of the race tests your mind even more than your muscle. Remember to stay poised, because if you panic and lose your head, you're not going to win, even if the other phases are executed perfectly.

At this point in the race, you feel fatigue. It's only natural. Sometimes runners lose their form and start to flail. Losing your form is just like stopping or even going backward. Just hold your course. Don't let your mind convince your body it's failing. Don't let it distract you from winning the prize.

Hold on to your faith. Believe you are doing all the right things, and it's going to pay off. At this point, all the hard work is done. You just need to hold on and trust the process. Regardless of the outcome, be grateful and proud of your results.

Pray—Silent and Constant Power

Prayer isn't a physical phase of the race that you practice. It's part of *every* phase.

Prayer shouldn't be something saved until the end when

you cry out, "God, please help me win." Talking to God is essential to the entire process of training and running the best race that you can. The beginning, middle, and end of every journey is richer and sweeter when shared with God.

When you pray you ask God to step in, and submit to His will. Through gratitude and admission, you ask Him to take your burdens away and trust that this is done.

Prayer frees you of worry, doubt, and fear.

Prayer fills you with hope and reminds you of your greater purpose. Not to win races or make more money, not to become CEO or president, but in all things serve and give glory to God.

Racing the 400-meters is so much like everyday life. It tests every part of us—our mind, body, and spirit. The most important thing you can do in the race of life is pray without ceasing (1 Thessalonians 5:17). Sometimes we might struggle to know what to pray for, or even how to pray, but constant communication with God is key.

Then you'll be able to fight through adversity, finish the race, keep your faith, and earn the greatest prize of all.

PUSH

Chase Your Dream

Chapter 1

CHAMPION GIRL

"For we are God's handiwork, created in Christ Jesus to do good works, which God prepared in advance for us to do."

—EPHESIANS 2:10

I'm the only one awake in my house. It's still dark outside, maybe six in the morning. I tiptoe around the bedroom carefully assembling my outfit, while trying not to wake my sister, Shari.

Socks match my tank top. Tank top matches my hair tie. Hair tie matches my wristband. I like to match.

"You're going to look pretty and run fast," Mom said the night before, as she labored over my stylish braids.

Noisy tree frogs drown out my footsteps as I make my way to my parents' bedroom. I'm nine years old, but I already know you have to dress up before you show up. Today I'll run in the biggest meet of the year—the Prep Champs. I'm all ready to go but somebody has to get up and drive me to the race.

"Baby, go back to sleep," Mom tells me from her pillow. "It's not time yet."

"I want to go now."

"Your race isn't until the afternoon," she insists. "You have all day to get ready."

Born to Run

Like most kids look forward to Christmas morning, I looked forward to track meets. The anticipation of racing was better than any present. Actually, it *was* a gift. A gift God gave me. He made me to run. And I got to open his gift every time I laced up my shoes.

Born in Kingston, Jamaica, I fell in love with track and field. Baseball may be America's pastime, but track and field rules Jamaica. Murals and statues of Merlene Ottey, Donald Quarrie, and Herb McKenley fill the landscape around Kingston. I knew their names and stories better than I knew the history of our Prime Minister. I wanted to be just like these track greats. I wanted *my* picture on a wall somewhere.

To me, there was no choice other than to run track. I started in elementary school, along with Shari. We went to a school called Vaz Prep. Every day after classes, we practiced on our school track.

Well, we called it a track. Really, it was just dirt and grass. There wasn't a rubber surface, or really even a track. Our coaches spray-painted the field with white lines, so it resembled a track. It wasn't much, but to me it was everything. I couldn't wait to get there.

Even the drills that marked the beginning of practice were fun. Before we started running, we would march in place as our arms shifted like perfect 90-degree levers. Then we'd do A Skips and B Skips. Throughout my running career, I never started a training session or lined up to race without warming up in the exact same order.

In A Skips, we'd bring our knees high into our chests as we pumped our arms and "skipped" down the track. The B Skips

HISTORY OF GREATNESS

For its size, no nation can compare with Jamaica when it comes to a history of greatness in track and field.

Merlene Ottey: When Ottey claimed bronze in the 200-meters at the 1980 Summer Olympics, she became the first English-speaking female athlete from the Caribbean to win an Olympic medal. She went on to compete in seven Olympics and win nine medals. Ottey has been called the "Queen of Track."

Donald Quarrie: Quarrie's statue greets people as they enter Jamaica's National Stadium. His performance at the 1976 Olympics in Montreal earned him worldwide fame as he took home the gold medal in the 100-meter dash and silver in the 200-meters.

Herb McKenley: McKenley was the world's fastest 400-meter runner in the late 1940s. He won a silver medal at the 1948 Summer Olympics. Then he earned a gold (in the 4x400 relay) and two silvers (400m and 100m) at the 1952 Olympics. After racing, he became a great coach and ambassador for Jamaican track and field.

were harder, because after bringing a knee to our chest, we'd kick it out before taking our next stride.

Those movements were an important part of my development. At the time, I didn't realize all the important muscle memory those drills taught me. I was just excited to find a sport I loved, to experience being good at something, and to discover a God-given talent.

I was fortunate to attend Vaz Prep, a high-quality school that also gave me access to great coaches. They set us up for success by teaching mechanics at a young age. No part of the race was overlooked. They even allowed us to practice on starting blocks, even though we couldn't use them in races until we were older.

Training with my friends was always a highlight. I begged my little sister to join track too. Shari, fifteen months my junior, was probably the faster of the two of us. My dad claimed she had better quick-twitch muscle fibers than I do. But Shari never showed much interest in running or racing.

While her track career was short-lived, Shari still came to all of my practices. She never complained about having to wait to do homework. After we'd finally come home and eat dinner, we didn't start studying until it was well past dark. Even though she was my little sister, Shari looked after me. She was always my quiet protector. Her constant presence lifted me, steadied me.

I've always been grateful for Shari. I did everything full steam ahead, unafraid of what might go wrong. If I was hanging upside down from the monkey bars, I'd try to swing too. Sure, I'd fall and hurt myself. But a few bruises and spills didn't stop me from moving forward, running toward whatever was next. And Shari was always there beside me.

Go Back to Go Forward

Every year, tens of thousands of people fill the national stadium in Kingston, Jamaica's capital, to watch kids ages seven to eleven run around a track. The Prep Champs are held to determine the country's best youth runners.

Fans from every school gather in packs in the bleachers, waving flags. They fill the thick, muggy air with drumbeats and rehearsed chants. At school in the days leading up to the meet, everybody would practice, usually riffing on whatever reggae song was popular at the moment.

"Vaz Prep a champion! Vaz Prep a champion!" I can hear that chant to this day.

By the time I competed in my third Prep Champs, there was already anticipation building about my potential. As a nine-year-old, my name and picture had appeared in the newspaper numerous times. People knew who I was and expected me to win, because that's what I did. I had never lost a race.

Wolmers, a neighboring elementary school, was our biggest rival. If the competition on the track was heated, it was just as hot in the stands. Schools occupied their own sections and baited each other with dueling chants.

"She can't beat our girls dis year," the legion of blue and

gold, the colors of Vaz Prep, proudly proclaimed in their customary Jamaican patois. "Sanya was the best last year, and she's the best again dis year."

A Vaz Prep chorus provided my walkout music.

"Sanya a champion! Sanya a champion!"

In that moment, I felt invincible.

I had already won a race earlier in the day—the 150-meters. But this race was *it*. The 60-meters determined the fastest girl. And that was me.

Our coaches didn't leave any part of the race to chance. They polished our technique. They methodically taught each aspect of sprinting—from starts to acceleration to leaning at the finish line.

Some of our opponents thought our starts were a little flashy. At Vaz Prep we were taught to begin by standing straight when the starter said, "On your mark." At "Set," we went down and touched the ground, sort of like an offensive lineman in football. Then we pushed off the line when we heard the gun. Maybe it was our coaches' way to gain an early edge on our competitors, but at the biggest meet of my young career, it nearly backfired.

During this race, the girl on my left was already down before I set. Then she shifted her position. That movement threw my concentration. Instead of going down and getting in my ready position, I rocked back. Just as I leaned back, the gun fired to start the race.

Bang!

Everyone surged into their sprints. I fell backward.

I'm going to lose, I thought.

In a 60-meter race, there isn't much time to make up for mistakes. When I finally bolted off the line, I was already behind by several yards.

It was the fastest I had ever run, an all-out crazy, furious pedaling to convert panic into power. My body felt numb. The shouts and support of the crowd went silent. My mind filled with a new thought: *I can't lose*. All I could see and feel was my lane and the finish line in front of me.

Run. Catch them. Keep running. Getting closer. Run. Move. Arms, Sanya, use your arms. Be strong. Ten meters to go. Almost there. Catch her. Run. There's the line. Another two steps. Reach. Get through the line. It's over.

I looked up at my dad. He sat in his usual spot above the finish line. I couldn't read his face. If he couldn't tell who won, nobody could. But whoever won had done so by an eyelash. It was a photo finish.

"Sanya a champion! Sanya a champion!" The chant rang out.

All I could do was hold back tears. I had blown it. I just knew it. I didn't deserve the cheers.

One of the longtime race officials, picked me up and hugged me as the group waited for the race result to be revealed.

"Great job," he told me. "Beautiful race."

Tears welled in my eyes and streamed down my cheeks.

"I think I lost," I told him.

"No, you won."

"Are you sure?"

"Yes, you won!"

A warm sense of relief rushed over me. The painful stiffness of worry released from my body. The official put me down, and I ran to my family for victory hugs.

"That's one of the best races I've ever seen!" Dad beamed. "I did not believe it was possible. How did you get your shoulder in front?"

I didn't have the answer. Everything was in a haze. Never before had my body been asked to shift so intensely. From a shaky start to a crazed sprint. From the panic of failure to the joy of victory.

"Sanya a champion! Sanya a champion!" the crowd continued chanting.

As the meet concluded, my family packed up and started walking to the parking lot. The field was being prepared for the final award presentation. I asked my dad to wait. Every year race organizers named a Champion Girl. If you won multiple races, you could earn that distinction. This year I thought I had a chance.

We were still in the bleachers when the voice came through

the speaker: "The Champion Girl in Class Two . . . is Sanya Richards."

My dad was so proud. He picked me up and lifted me over the fence and onto the track. I ran over to accept the award. I was elated, and so was my family, to be recognized as the best in the whole class.

From then on, if there was a trophy I could get, I went for it.

SANYA SAYS

To go forward, I had to first go backward. That's not how my coaches taught it at practice. But the lesson burns in my memory. Everything doesn't always work as planned. When plans fail, you can't give up. You have to trust and keep moving forward.

The start is important, but what matters most is the finish.

Chapter 2

RUNS IN THE FAMILY

"See what great love the Father has lavished
on us, that we should be called children
of God! And that is what we are!"

—1 JOHN 3:1

I first competed in the Preps Champs when I was seven. I already loved running, but after that first meet I was hooked for life. The enormity of the event charged my body with adrenaline. Imagine a carnival inside a track meet. That's the energy of the stadium. I was anxious, but mostly excited to race and to win . . . which I did.

The next year, Dad picked up a program and looked through all the times. My father, Archie Richards, never lacked vision and a plan to accomplish it. He quickly noticed that my times in the youngest class were faster than the boys in the same age group. In fact, my times were as good as girls a year or two older than me. He didn't tell me until a few years later, but Dad realized then that I had a special gift and made the decision to nurture my talent.

My mom, Sharon, likes to stay levelheaded, but she delights in our family. She believed in what Dad thought was possible. She was passionate about us girls following what we loved. So she, and everyone in my family, bought into my running dreams.

Dad, Mom, and Shari were my first entourage. I always felt strengthened by the support of my family. Walking into track meets, with the three of them around me, I felt unbeatable. That attitude helps in track, because the competition really begins before you set your feet in the blocks and brace for the gun. Racers size each other up by their body language. *How confident do they look? How do they warm-up?* Track is as pure as it gets—me against you. But with my family behind me, it was *all* of Team Richards against *you*. We all knew what we came to do. Line up and win.

Dad was our flag-bearer. He led the way and set the tone. He decided early on that reviewing races on film would be essential to my development. He went out and bought a video camera, so he could tape all my competitions. That meant he had to have the perfect view, perched right above the finish line. He would ignore stern instructions or bulldoze his way in if he needed to. He never planned to stay in his perfect spot for the entire meet, but he *had* to get my race on tape. No one could stop him.

That dedication, paired with his inspirational words and constant encouragement, made me feel like I could win a race running backwards.

Mom and Shari evened me out. I could always count on Mom to be polite, graceful, and greet everyone with a quiet smile. She kept me calm.

"Be easy, Sanya," she'd say in her Jamaican accent. "Don't get crazy, Sanya. Just win the race."

Shari was my backbone. She reminded me of my hard work and preparation, confirming that I was a winner. Before every race, it was her voice that would start me as much as the gun.

To me, every race began the same way.

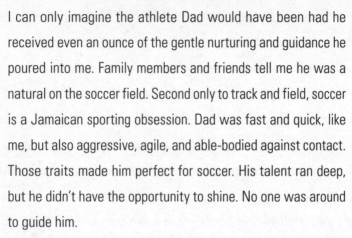

IN MY FATHER'S STEPS

I can only imagine the athlete Dad would have been had he received even an ounce of the gentle nurturing and guidance he poured into me. Family members and friends tell me he was a natural on the soccer field. Second only to track and field, soccer is a Jamaican sporting obsession. Dad was fast and quick, like me, but also aggressive, agile, and able-bodied against contact. Those traits made him perfect for soccer. His talent ran deep, but he didn't have the opportunity to shine. No one was around to guide him.

In fact, some of the only guidance he ever received was bad advice. He was told to not lift weights. Strength training was presumed to hinder speed. That's a statement I can testify to as being completely false. Yet as a young man, Dad had no way of knowing. He eventually settled on soccer and other sports being just hobbies. But he vowed if he ever had children with an inclination toward athletics, he would fight to not only protect it, but promote it.

First, silence would envelope the stadium. Still and quiet, the entire crowd would hold its breath.

Then the starter's voice would ring out.

"On your mark."

"Set."

Bang!

As soon as the pistol popped, one noise would reach above the din.

"LET'S GO SANYA!"

That's my Shari. She used the loudest voice she could muster to reach down from the stands, lift me out of the blocks, and push me out around the track. When I watch recordings of my professional races now—nationally broadcasted meets in packed stadiums—I can still hear Shari.

But Team Richards didn't stop there. My aunt Claire and cousin Yollie had moved to Maryland when I was a toddler. Every summer they'd fly back to Jamaica to watch me run. Then there was Aunt Maureen, Uncle Tony, Aunt Althea, and my other cousins. Not a lot of people can say that when they were a child their family flew in from another country to watch them run. But mine did. They believed in me. My personal cheering section filled any stadium with their shouts and excitement.

My family's foundation solidified my confidence. In Jamaica, that was essential, because winning is prized. Losing is an embarrassment. You're either first or you're last. There's no in between.

At age seven, I won the very first race I ever entered and my taste for winning was established. I always wanted more.

But I knew there was no easy path to the podium. Victory took effort, and I was happy to do the hard work to keep on winning.

Film Study

"You're going to be the best in the world."

Those were my dad's words to me when I was still in grade school. Eventually, I believed him. When I was nine, I wrote in a school assignment that I would be an Olympic champion.

He knew to get serious about training and racing, I had to want to get serious. He couldn't push me to greatness, it had to be my idea. I had to be willing to work for it.

Dad knew the best way for me to believe was to see results. That's why he videotaped all my races. Every night after my meets, we'd plug the tape into the VCR and watch the race on our TV. Over and over—seven, eight, nine times—we'd watch me run the race. The first three or four times, we'd just relive the moments and celebrate what I did right. My dad couldn't have been more supportive.

"Beautiful, darling," he'd say. "That's great, baby."

One of my favorite parts of the videos was when Dad would turn the camera around after I finished my race and show my family. My mom, sister, aunts, uncles, cousins—all of them would be going *crazy* in the stands. As a young girl, when I saw how happy my success made them, it inspired me.

My family's excitement was a driving force in making me want to pursue track and field further.

Then the last couple of times through the tape, Dad would critique me. No matter how much I'd won by, or what the clock said, there was a part of the race I could've executed better. We'd look at my starts, how my arms and hands could have more powerfully worked in unison with my legs to pull me to top speed, or how my right leg was always a little crooked coming out of the block—a quirk that still showed in my Olympic victory.

Dad's method was masterful. He never caused me to dwell on a mistake or look back. We appreciated that I had gotten out there and given my best. We celebrated what was accomplished. Then we flipped the switch to what was next. Eyes up, head up, looking forward to another goal.

As Dad and I focused on maximizing my physical and mental potential, Mom was also putting together a plan to put me on the path to success. Specifically, my path to higher education.

Mom already had family members living in the United States. Her sister had relocated from Jamaica to the Fort Lauderdale area in Florida. Though my education in Jamaica was top-notch, Mom knew more scholarship opportunities would be available for me to attend an American university if I attended high school in America.

It took some convincing, especially for Dad, before our

family made the decision to move to Florida. But eventually Dad agreed with the reasoning. He knew I could better compete for academic and athletic scholarships to get a college education if we were living in the United Stated. Plus, our new home would be only an hour-and-a-half flight from Jamaica.

So when I was twelve, my family and I left everything we knew in Jamaica and made a leap of faith.

SANYA SAYS

From the minute Dad looked through the Prep Champs program and realized I had the potential to be great, he began learning everything he could about sprinting. He studied the champions, memorized their strategies and times, and knew age-group records. That helped him establish goals and benchmarks for my running career.

Every time I achieved one of the goals we set, it energized me. By making and meeting goals, it reinforced in my own mind what could be accomplished with hard work.

No matter what you hope to accomplish in life, it's important to educate yourself and make a plan. The Bible tells us, "The plans of the diligent lead to profit" (Proverbs 21:5). By consistently working toward a goal, you'll see God do big things in your life.

Chapter 3

COMING TO AMERICA

"I am with you and will watch over you
wherever you go, and I will bring you back
to this land. I will not leave you until I
have done what I have promised you."

—GENESIS 28:15

The transition to America wasn't easy. New home. New school. New country. It helped having family already in the area. But the differences between Jamaica and the United States were everywhere, especially at school.

In Jamaica we wore uniforms, but in my new school, we could choose to wear any outfit we wanted. I freaked out. For a week, I tried on everything in my closet. Finally, I settled on my first-day outfit: a denim dress with white Chuck Taylors.

Pines Middle School was located between Fort Lauderdale and Miami. With around 1,200 students, it was about the same size as Vaz Prep. But that's where the similarities ended. When I arrived on campus for the first time, I was excited, anxious, and nervous.

Some of those feelings went away when I immediately got a compliment from one of my classmates on my sneakers.

Thank you, God, I thought. *Things are going to be great.*

For a few moments, I believed I had nothing to worry about. I had no problem finding my classroom and getting a seat. But as quickly as I felt like I fit in, I made a social blunder that showed I still had a lot to learn about my new country.

In Jamaica it was customary to stand when your teacher walked in and to say, "Good morning." So when I saw the teacher, I stood and started to speak. That's when I realized no one else was standing.

I was so embarrassed. All the kids looked at me like I was some foreigner, standing all alone. I quickly sat back down and avoided eye contact. *Yes, Sanya,* I thought. *You're no longer in Jamaica.*

I couldn't wait for lunchtime. As soon as the bell rang, I made a beeline for the cafeteria. I scanned the room for a familiar face. Shari smiled back at me. I sat down with her and shared what had happened that morning. She almost cried she was laughing so hard.

Her laughter made me laugh too. Shari hadn't made the same mistake. She was clever enough to wait patiently in her seat to see what the other kids would do when the teacher walked in. By observing the situation, she avoided the embarrassment I had endured.

I was used to being a leader. I thought leaders didn't wait— they led. They plowed forward and everybody followed them. At Vaz Prep, I had always been voted the class captain by my classmates. Now I had to learn the best leaders must know where they're going *before* taking the lead. A good leader waits, learns, and spends time following as well as leading.

Shari and I were best friends already. But our bond intensified in America. Early on, we only had each other. With our thick accents and different traditions, we really stood out.

I also stood out on the track—in a good way. As soon as track season started, I went out for the team. This was the place where I felt most confident. I knew I could help my school. I made the team and a lot of new friends.

KNOW DIFFERENT

The island nation of Jamaica could fit in the state of Florida thirteen times! And Jamaica's population of 2.8 million people is only a fraction of the 20 million in Florida. While the temperatures are about the same in Southern Florida and Jamaica, there are plenty of differences.

OFFICIAL LANGUAGE

Jamaica: English and Jamaican Patois (an English-based language that also uses words from West Africa, Spain, and the Caribbean)

Florida: English

OFFICIAL BIRD

Jamaica: Doctor Bird, also called swallowtail humming bird

Florida: Northern mockingbird

OFFICIAL FRUIT

Jamaica: Ackee

Florida: Orange

MOST POPULAR SPORTS

Jamaica: Soccer, track and field, cricket

Florida: Football, baseball

Even with all my new track friends, Shari stayed my best friend. We shared a bedroom in our family's first small apartment in Florida. And even after we eventually settled into a bigger home, we remained close.

No matter what school we attended, Shari and I knew we'd have at least one friend, because the other would be there. Shari always looked after me, but I was still the big sister. I needed to know everything was good with her. Even if we didn't share the same lunchtime, I went to the school cafeteria to check on her every day. Sometimes I'd have to make up an excuse to leave class, but it was important to me to know that she was okay, had friends, and was having a good day.

That's just what sisters do.

Faithful Family

I grew up knowing *about* God, but I didn't accepted Christ as my personal Savior until I turned thirteen.

My aunt Maureen could always be found at the Caribbean Baptist Church (now known as ChristWay Baptist) in Miramar, Florida. She would take Shari and me to church every Thursday for choir practice and each Sunday for service. I loved it.

Aunt Maureen's faith was contagious. She loved Jesus! And Caribbean Baptist felt like a safe community. I didn't feel like I was competing. Everyone was proud of me for being me. They loved me unconditionally, just like God does.

The message of Jesus and how he died for me began to sink

into my heart. After a year of going to church with my aunt, I was saved and baptized during a church service.

Aunt Maureen didn't just play a part in my coming to America and coming to Christ. She helped my parents research possible locations for our new home. Because she'd lived in the area for a while and knew the neighborhoods, we trusted her guidance. She was also the first person to open our eyes to St. Thomas Aquinas High School.

The first time I visited St. Thomas Aquinas I wanted to be a part of its history of excellence. The Raiders had won more than 100 Florida state championships in sports, and I hoped to add to that total.

What started as a small, private Catholic school in 1936 had grown to a campus covering almost 30 acres in urban Fort Lauderdale. The classrooms and laboratories were state-of-the-art. The college preparatory courses were challenging, demanding the best from students. The athletic facilities were more like a small college's than a high school's. And best of all, the Raiders' colors were blue and gold—just like Vaz Prep.

It turned out to be a perfect spot for my continued growth as a student and as a competitor.

With all the positives of attending St. Thomas Aquinas, there was one difference between schools in Jamaica and America that was difficult to ignore. As a young Jamaican, I was used to living in a community where most of the people looked just like me. Most of the students I went to school with, and individuals I interacted with in Jamaica were black. At St. Thomas Aquinas, a majority of the kids were white. Now I was in the minority.

I've heard many people say they don't see color, and it usually makes me skeptical. But I can honestly say as one of the youngest students in my grade, I never felt like I was any different. I always felt included and had lots of friends—both inside and outside of sports.

To me, the culture gap that took the longest to adjust to was on the track. In Jamaica, second-place is just another name for first loser. There's no way around it. But at my first track meet at St. Thomas Aquinas, I was more than a little taken aback when one of my teammates was finishing a race far in back of the pack. As she rounded the last turn, people clapped furiously and shouted their support.

"Come on!" they shouted as she hustled toward the finish line. "You got this!"

What in the world? I thought. *She's behind. She's losing.*

Then it hit me: Leaving it all on the track was deserving of a crowd's appreciation.

Almost immediately my mindset started to change.

SANYA SAYS

In Jamaica, there's no such thing as a participation ribbon. It's all about winning. So it took me a little while to understand that you can be satisfied at the end of a competition if you don't win but give your best effort.

God wants you to compete in such a way as to win the prize. But you can't—and won't—win every time. Recognize God's plan and honor him no matter the outcome. When you've given your all, you can learn from and benefit from both victory and defeat.

Chapter 4

RISING STAR

"I will exalt you, Lord, for you lifted me out of the depths and did not let my enemies gloat over me."

—PSALM 30:1

D espite my early sports triumphs in Jamaica, I was virtually unknown in Florida. By the end of my freshman year at St. Thomas Aquinas, that started to change. I competed in five events at the state track and field championships—the 100- and 200-meter races, long jump, high jump, and 4x400 relay.

I still loved being the fastest girl and won the 100m and 200m races in record-setting times.

Competing in five events, including the preliminary rounds, took everything I could muster. But I was happy to stretch myself thin, because that's what the team needed. We won the Class 5A state championship that year. Actually, we won four-straight state titles during my high school career from 1999–2002.

The Florida Sun-Sentinel named me its female track athlete of the year, making me one of the youngest to ever receive the honor. Soon people outside of Florida were starting to hear my name too.

National Stage

By the time I was 16, my family was fully settled in the Sunshine State. I had made strong friendships, thanks mostly to the camaraderie of teammates.

On the track, things were going even better. I was earning attention for my form and race times, competing all across the country.

After one summer club meet, a woman approached me. She

introduced herself as Joy Kimani and encouraged me to register and compete with the junior national team. I was ecstatic. In track and field, running for your country represents the pinnacle of the sport. You just don't bring honor to yourself, you bring it to your country.

Think about it: When you win the Olympics, they don't play your favorite song on the medal stand. They play the National Anthem. I couldn't wait to go sign up.

But when my mom and I went to register for the national team, we ran into an unexpected problem.

"We'll need your passport, please."

We should've anticipated the request, but we hadn't. I turned to my mom as we realized immediately that we didn't have one. We were legal immigrants with a green card to live in the United States. But we weren't naturalized citizens. If I wanted to be on Team USA, it would be a process.

Barely legal to drive a car, I was faced with a choice I never imagined making. Jamaica or the United States? At the time, I could only legally run for Jamaica. I wanted to compete for Team USA. All my friends were American, and I wanted to make the team with them. I'd lived in Florida for four years. That felt like a lifetime. I didn't know any of the young Jamaican athletes anymore. I begged my parents to let me join the US team. They had many discussions about it. We were and still are proud Jamaicans, but ultimately my parents thought it was the best decision for me and my future to run for the United States.

My mom started working toward her citizenship immediately. Once she was naturalized, Shari and I would automatically become US citizens because we were minors. Then I'd be eligible to compete for the United States at international meets.

We quickly learned becoming a US citizen is a tough process. I started quizzing Mom, a complete change from the norm. She usually helped me with my homework. Now I was helping her with American history. My mom was making a huge commitment for me, and I wanted to be there for her as much as I could. I was elated when she passed all the tests and we became US citizens during my senior year in 2002.

No Class

Every student looks forward to her last year of high school, and I was no different. Track and field had brought me a lot of attention and success. It felt great being known around campus, because I always loved people and went out of my way to make friends. Not just the people on the track team but everybody.

If you were in my class, in the cafeteria, or even in the parking garage when I pulled up, I wanted to get to know you. It was fair to say I was one of the most popular girls at school. Add a 4.0 GPA, and I had struck the perfect balance as a well-rounded student-athlete. At least I thought so.

Before the summer of my senior year, I attended the junior Olympics with one of my favorite teammates. I shared with her about a new crush I had and how I hoped we would start dating. He was the most popular guy in school and on the football team. Gregarious, handsome, and funny—all the girls liked him.

Turned out, she did too.

As I walked the hallways on the first day of school, I saw the teammate I had confided in, holding my crush's hand. My chest tightened and my breathing shortened. I was in utter shock.

How could this be? I thought. *When had this happened and why hadn't she told me?*

I was heartbroken.

After being blindsided by my teammate, the dynamic of my circle of friends changed. Most of the student body was unaware of what happened, but my once close group of friends who sat and visited on the stairs after class was now divided. Friendships fractured as people chose sides.

Because I cherished my friendships, I struggled with the ever-present tension that filled the school hallways. No longer able to speak to old friends freely or hang out the way we once had, I was always on guard. I continued to excel on the track and in the classroom, but my social life was in shambles.

One morning, between homeroom and first period, Shari and two of our closest friends, Raecena and Nicole, were chatting before class. One of the guys on the football team, walked by and mumbled a sly comment under his breath. Shari and Raecena, the wittiest of my group, snapped back at him. I never said a word. But out of nowhere, he spun around and took his anger out on me.

His rage was both unexpected and frightening. Suddenly, he punched me in the face. We couldn't believe it. Before I could say anything or retaliate, people jumped in and separated us.

Everything happened in such a flurry. I had to call my dad. I could feel his outrage through the phone. He hadn't even heard the full story before he was parked on campus. By the time he arrived, the young man was long gone—expelled from school.

It was probably the worst experience of my high school days. But my family kept me going. They supported me and encouraged me to stay involved in the church. I started to understand that being a Christian doesn't exclude you from tough times and trials but, rather, invites Christ to walk on the journey with you.

Race of My Life

By the end of my high school running career, I had broken school records and helped lead the St. Thomas Aquinas Raiders to three straight state championships. I was nearly unbeatable in the 100- and 200-meters. But I still wanted more.

COURTED BY COLLEGES

Colleges identify the top athletes early on in high school. Through summer leagues, state championships, and raw statistics, the best athletes are then courted by the top universities. Based on my excellence on the track and in the classroom, I had college coaches visit me every weekend. It was a family dream realized and a big part of why we moved to the United States.

Coaches visited from all over the country—Stanford, LSU, South Carolina, Miami, Florida, Tennessee, and many others. LSU had won the most national titles. But all along my favorite was coach Beverly Kearney from the University of Texas. Her 100-watt smile, her swag and confidence, and her young, talented team seemed like the perfect fit for me. So I signed up to be a Texas Longhorn.

Maybe it was a fluke or maybe fate—but my senior year was the first time I ran the 400-meters in competition. I took to it like Cinderella to the glass slipper. It just fit.

At the National Scholastic Indoor Championships, I set a new national record in the quarter mile, shaving more than a second off the previous mark. I had gone there focused on the 200m title and record, both of which I attained, but my performance in the 400m opened my eyes to the potential and possibility of a different race.

The high school track season flew by. As I entered the state championships, front-page photos and big headlines felt like the norm. I may have started out as an unknown freshman, but now I was the one to beat.

To excel in anything, you have to have confidence. My confidence came from God and knowing the hard work that I put in during training would pay off. I never shied away from boldly stating my goals, and the newspaper reporters gladly quoted me. Everyone knew I entered the state meet my senior year chasing new state records in the 100m, 200m, and 400m.

I ended up winning all three events. I even established a new Florida state record in the 400-meters. But I hadn't accomplished everything I set out to do. Silently, I was satisfied. I knew the challenge my body was undertaking, competing in so many events.

Through my efforts, I had led the Raiders to a fourth-straight team title and become the second runner ever to sweep the 100-meters four-straight times. And my nine individual titles still placed me in the top-ten all-time for female athletes in Florida history.

Now high school was over and even bigger challenges lay ahead.

SANYA SAYS

Right before my senior year, I injured my leg and ended up losing two races at the national prep outdoor meet. During the ride home with my dad after my final training session, he asked me, "Do you want to be the best?"

I thought about it for the rest of the ride. When we got home, I told my dad, "I am willing to do whatever it takes to be the best."

Almost immediately, he turned our garage into a weight room. My mom, who had been a gym instructor in Jamaica, created a workout routine for me. Dad had me do 1,000 sit-ups every day. I'd go to the track before everyone else and run stadium stairs. I studied recordings of my races. Even my diet changed. No more junk food. It was all chicken, fish, and vegetables.

I became a true student of my sport and learned how to help my body perform at its best.

Sometimes, to chase your dreams, you need to push yourself physically to prepare yourself mentally for the obstacles that will come.

Chapter 5

NO BREAK FOR SUMMER

"We do not want you to become lazy, but to imitate those who through faith and patience inherit what has been promised."

—HEBREWS 6:12

The summer of 2002 gave me a glimpse into the future. Since I was a child, my family had helped me dream of what it'd be like to compete against the world's best. Those months between high school graduation and enrolling as a freshman at the University of Texas allowed me to completely focus on track. No homework. No group projects. The only thing that required my attention was running.

As my focus intensified, so did the pressure. My family traveled to Eugene, Oregon for the first time, for the prestigious Prefontaine Classic. It was probably the first meet that Dad didn't direct himself to a seat above the finish line. At the largest one-day track meet in the United States, he didn't have to worry about making his own recording. It was on TV, broadcast nationally by ESPN2. And I was the only high schooler invited.

Historic Hayward Field on the campus of the University of Oregon quickly earned a special place in my heart. I held the fastest high school girls' 400-meter time in the nation. My indoor performances that year in the 400m and 200m would have placed me among the top five against the top collegiate runners.

Just a few weeks prior to the Prefontaine Classic, I had set a new Florida state record in the 400-meters at 52.51 seconds. Chasing the national record of 50.74 was the next goal. Dad always had me looking forward, asking what's next and what's possible.

The field featured two Olympians and a handful of other

world-class, professional runners. With so many big names, I was back to being a nobody. I wasn't expected to do any better than finish last.

Winning wasn't my goal. I knew that'd be nearly impossible. But breaking the national junior record was in my sights. In 2000, Monique Henderson had run 50.74 to set the mark. Now I wanted to break it. By setting a goal, I was able to stay motivated to be at my best.

The event opened my eyes to how big an opportunity I had in sports. When Dad and I first walked onto the track for practice, I saw Olympic stars such as sprinters Gail Devers and Marion Jones, and pole vaulter Stacy Dragila.

"Dad, this is it," I said. "We're finally here. This is what we've been working toward."

He could hardly contain his pride. He stayed equally proud of me after the 400m race, even though I fell short of the national record. I ran 51.15. But I surprised everyone with a second-place finish out of lane 2. (The winner was eventually banned from the sport a year later for steroid use.)

Following the race, the announcer called me back onto the track and urged me to take a victory lap. The Hayward Field crowd, some of the biggest track fans in the world, stood and applauded.

I was stunned. They were cheering for me . . . after I finished *second*.

Only in America.

Last Chance

My busy summer of racing continued at the Junior National Championships at Stanford University. I competed in the 200- and 400-meters. The 200m finals came first. The field was packed with speed, including Allyson Felix—a young up-and-coming phenom. The race was one of the closest of my career as I edged out Allyson to win by three-hundredths of a second.

Riding a wave of confidence, I came back the next day in the 400m finals. It was a beautiful June afternoon in northern California. The stands were packed. I was so excited to run, especially because Monique Henderson was one of the athletes in the finals.

Because Monique was in college, I had never raced against her. I had only run with her junior record of 50.74 in my mind. Seeing her in person made it all the more real.

I don't know if it was the weather, my attitude, or having Monique in the field, but I ran the perfect race. I won with a time of 50.69 and broke the junior record! Monique finished right behind me. She was so gracious, giving me a hug and congratulating me on the record.

I quickly ran over to the stands where my mom, dad, and sister were going wild. They knew it had been my last chance to break the junior record in the 400—a record that still stands today.

Hurtful Homecoming

Another huge meet awaited me in July. For the first time, the IAAF World Junior Championships were held at the national stadium in Kingston, Jamaica.

My Team USA international debut would be on a stage where I already had so many cherished memories. This country—this track—helped shape me as a runner and competitor. I loved my home country, and I anxiously awaited a happy homecoming.

The Jamaican people, though, felt as if I had abandoned my homeland. Instead of warmth and affection, hostility greeted me as I arrived in Jamaica. I hoped for appreciation. I received resentment. At a press conference to preview the star-studded championships, I could feel my nerves fraying. "I hope everybody will still love me," one newspaper quoted me as saying.

Like usual, I carried a heavy load for my team. The coaches scheduled me to run the 200m and 400m as well as the 4x100 and 4x400 relays. The entire junior squad voted me team captain and elected me to be the flag bearer during the opening ceremonies. I was honored to be both, but told my teammates I didn't want to offend the Jamaican fans. I declined being Team USA's flag bearer.

Still, the locals suggested I was a traitor. Boos and jeers

MY OVAL OFFICE

The Oval Office is the name of the official office of the President of the United States. Located in the West Wing of the White House, it's where the president does all his official business.

My official business was conducted on a 400-meter oval track. Because I spent so much time running around an oval, I started calling the track my "oval office."

rang out as I arrived at the stadium. I was caught off guard. Emotionally, I wasn't prepared for the negativity. Shari cried in the stands.

As ugly as my reception was from the crowd, the Jamaicans couldn't contain their excitement about an up-and-coming sprinter named Usain Bolt. At 15, he thrilled the hometown fans by winning the 200m—making him the youngest sprinter in history to win a gold at the World Junior Championships.

While Usain was making history, I wished the meet *was* history. The opening heat of the 200m was scheduled just hours before the 400-meter final. In these opening heats, all you have to do is finish among the top two to advance to the next round. Maybe it was being in that stadium. Maybe I wanted to show the crowd that I was still the best. Or maybe I was a young runner with a lot to learn about racing with strategy. But the win-or-lose mentality that years of Jamaican track training ingrained within me reared its ugly head.

I bolted out of the blocks as the starting gun went off. Only a girl from Canada stayed with me. She ran the race of her life. I had to set a personal best to beat her—in the first round.

We were so far in front of the rest of the field that I could have geared back, walked the final meters, and still moved on. But I was consumed with having to win, and that obsession came back to beat me.

The 400-meter final was a sight to be seen. More than 15,000 fans crammed inside National Stadium. Steel drum beats and the black, green, and gold flags of Jamaica rose into the muggy night air from a sea of people. Every fan wanted to see the Jamaicans win. Unlike my Vaz Prep days, I was not in the right colors. They even taunted my family.

"She nah go win!"

"She's a sellout. She don't deserve di gold."

Even though I was treated as the villain, my focus didn't waver. This time, like every time I entered a race, I was set on winning. My mind and heart were ready.

Bang!

I ran out hard and felt strong.

But when I came into the last 100 meters, there was nothing left. My energy was gone, drained out of me on the same spot where only a few hours earlier I used that crazy kick to conquer my 200m qualifying heat. Now when it mattered in the 400m final—when a winner was actually determined—my legs couldn't answer when my mind called for them to kick it in.

I looked over at my American teammate Monique Henderson in disappointment as she passed me. I couldn't find another gear to match her speed in the final 100 meters. I was devastated.

Just past the finish line, I found Monique and hugged her in congratulations. Then I found a nearby chair and slumped into it. I was exhausted and humiliated. As I stared at the track, I criticized my effort. I had wanted to win. I had wanted to set a personal record. I wanted to prove to the Jamaican fans that I lived up to my billing. But I hadn't done any of that.

I went down to Jamaica with my sights set on a pair of individual gold medals. I left without any. With a silver medal in the 400m and bronze in the 200m, I was beaten, mentally and physically.

Then to add insult to injury, I sprained my ankle during a preliminary heat of the 4x400 relay. I wasn't even supposed to compete in the race. I was in the stands in my jeans and T-shirt, supporting one of my teammates, when I was asked to fill in. I didn't even have my uniform or spikes. I borrowed some, and after crossing the finish line in first place, I stepped into a covered hole and severely rolled my ankle.

It was a difficult international debut to say the least, but my parents ensured I didn't leave our native land on a bad note. Some of my fondest family memories growing up were spent on Hellshire Beach. Famous for its fried escoveitch fish—a spicy and peppery Jamaican treat that's always eaten around Easter— and warm water, Hellshire Beach was the perfect escape. My family took me there for some food and relaxation. It was easy to forget about my performances when I was surrounded by tropical beauty and my family. I needed that to help reset ... I had new goals to pursue.

Day to Remember

Later that month, all I could think about was college. I couldn't wait to move to Austin, Texas, and start life as a collegiate athlete. I was still a little bummed about the trip to Jamaica. But my dad was good at getting me to learn from the past without dwelling on it.

My dad always told me, "The only way the past can benefit the future is if you learn from it." If I stayed down or disappointed, I would take that energy to my next competition. That would only hold me back, because every race was a new opportunity to reach my goals.

One afternoon as I dreamed about life at the University of Texas, my mom interrupted my thoughts and reminded me about a photo shoot for a local newspaper. I put on one of my best outfits and hurried to the car. We drove to a hotel near Miami. Rushing inside, I saw one of my uncles in the hallway.

What's he doing at my photo shoot? I wondered. I soon found out when the doors to the ballroom opened. Instead of a backdrop, lights, and cameras, a room full of people turned and applauded for me. The St. Thomas Aquinas athletics director, George Smith, and my high school coach, John Guarino, organized the surprise event to honor me as the 2002 Gatorade National High School Girls Athlete of the Year.

I became Florida's first track and field student-athlete to earn national athlete of the year, joining other Floridians like Alex Rodriguez and Emmitt Smith who had also received the award.

But there was an even bigger surprise. It was Sanya Richards Day!

According to a proclamation signed by our congressman and a commendation from the city of Fort Lauderdale, July 25, 2002, was officially named Sanya Richards Day. I could barely believe it. Jeb Bush, Florida's then governor, had even sent a congratulatory letter.

Not only was it the greatest honor of my young career, it also motivated me to live up to expectations. The people who chose me for those awards believed in my ability to move on and establish myself among the greats.

SANYA SAYS

It doesn't pay off to get stuck. Why worry about what *was?* For me, it was always best to flip the dial and ask: *What is to come?*

That thinking was what pulled me out of the negative experience I had had in Jamaica at the 2002 World Junior Championships. Dealing with the crowd and the losses could've been devastating. But I was always looking forward.

Eventually, I saw the Jamaicans' jeers as coming from a loving place. They were disappointed because I wasn't competing for the country of my birth. Today, it's not a negative memory in my mind, even though it was a tough experience being on the receiving end of so much disapproval. I learned compassion by experiencing the opposite.

To push forward, you can't waste energy being upset, dwelling on disappointment, or looking for differences. Instead, embrace the similarities of people around you. When we accept Christ, we all become children of God. In that, we're all the same—regardless of where we were born, where we live, or what we look like.

Chapter 6

DON'T MESS WITH TEXAS

"For I know the plans I have for you," declares
the L ORD, *"plans to prosper you and not to harm
you, plans to give you hope and a future."*

—JEREMIAH 29:11

When I arrived at the University of Texas campus, I was over the moon. I couldn't wait to join the powerhouse Lady Longhorns' track and field team. Texas had won national championships in 1998 and 1999, and I wanted to bring that glory back to Austin.

"The winning tradition of the Texas Longhorns will not be entrusted to the weak or the timid." The first time I walked into the weight room and saw those words etched on the back wall, I knew I was in the right place.

I felt at home in Texas from the moment I took my official visit as a junior in high school. The Lady Longhorns were welcoming and friendly, and Raasin McIntosh and Nichole Denby hosted me on campus.

Talk about opposites: Raasin the hyper, fun, crazy girl from Houston and Nichole the calm, cool, and collected girl from California. Their personalities were different, but their work ethic and commitment to track were identical. I just knew I wanted to be their teammates.

From my first visit, we formed an unbreakable bond, which helped us push each other during practice and in competition.

Then there was our coach, Beverly Kearney. She was one of only two female African American Division I head coaches in track and field. I admired that. Until college, most of my coaches had been male. Aside from Mrs. June Simpson, one of my very first coaches in Jamaica, men had always coached me.

Mom and Dad gushed about this opportunity to learn from Bev. Her larger-than-life personality and desire to win made her someone I wanted to be around, someone I could relate to, and someone I could aspire to be like. A sharp dresser and slick talker, Bev's aura was so mesmerizing she could convince you of anything. Her charismatic style mimicked a preacher's. Sometimes she'd fire us up by holding an hour-long team meeting in the middle of practice.

"If they aren't in burnt orange and they can't score us any points, we don't speak or interact with them," Bev would say. "When we enter a competition, we're on a mission. It starts the moment you walk in the arena."

Bold in burnt orange, with *Texas* across our chests, we were a sight to see and a force to be reckoned with. Always well-dressed, we held our heads high and focused our eyes forward. No one messed with us. We were the fierce girls of college track and field, and we owned it. We wanted to get in our opponents' heads before we ever lined up to race. We were "Bev's girls," and we were proud of it.

National Stage

I had chosen to run for the Lady Longhorns because I thought we could win a national championship. And it looked like we might accomplish that goal at the end of my freshman year.

We had a dominant season. Going into the NCAA Track

BEST FIRST DATE EVER

Everything didn't always work out the way I dreamed at the University of Texas, but I did meet the man of my dreams there. One evening, I saw Aaron Ross in a campus cafeteria and called him over. He was on the football team, and I was on the track team. As student-athletes at a big university, we both had demanding schedules.

We started talking, and he asked me out. He took me to dinner on Saturday night and to church the very next day. I guess you could say the rest is history. In that brief amount of time, I knew he was the one. He encouraged me to follow my dreams, and I encouraged him to pursue his goal of playing in the NFL.

and Field championships, we were on a roll. We had won the Big 12 Conference championships at our home stadium with me and Raasin leading the way. Each of us scored 22.5 points for our team, more than any other athlete—male or female—at the meet.

So when we arrived at Sacramento State on June 11, 2003, our confidence was riding high. Personally, I picked up where I had left off in high school by winning a national title. I took first in the 400-meters, edging out DeeDee Trotter of Tennessee. Then Keisha Downer, Moushaumi Robinson, Raasin, and I combined to win the 4x400 relay. Those were Texas' only two victories in the meet, which was actually one more victory than LSU had.

But the Tigers had more depth, and they finished second in three events. LSU ended the meet with 64 points for its thirteenth title in women's track and field. We scored 50 points to take second.

Being so close to the top made us hungrier than ever to win it all at the 2004 NCAA Track and Field championships. Texas hosted the event, and we were all so excited. With home-field advantage, we pictured ourselves holding up the championship trophy.

We had one of the best teams in the country. I had the fastest time in the nation in the 400-meters. Raasin was favored to win the 400 hurdles, and Nichole was a top bid for the 100 hurdles. With the three of us leading the team, we knew victory was within reach.

But quickly, the championship started to slip from our grasp. Everything that could go wrong, did go wrong. Our 4x100 relay team easily qualified for the finals . . . or so we thought. After I helped anchor the team, judges came forward and disqualified the squad on the weirdest technicality.

It had rained during the event. While the other schools used white tape as markers on the track, Bev gave us yellow tennis balls cut in half to use as our markers. We all thought it was legal. Later, we discovered the judges ruled that it gave us an unfair advantage under the conditions.

We were counting on those ten points. Then, like dominoes, we all just started crashing down. Raasin hit a hurdle in her race and finished fourth. I placed third in the 400, behind DeeDee Trotter of Tennessee and Monique Henderson of UCLA. Then our team fell down in the 4x400 relay finals. We had qualified first in the event. With the fall, we took sixth. It was a nightmare.

But there was one shining light. Nichole, my best friend, won the 100 hurdles.

As a standout in high school, she ran well in college but had never won a national title. It was her senior year and her last chance. She ran the best race of the night for the Lady Longhorns and set a new meet record. Although I was upset about my performance, I was happy for Nichole. She had worked so hard and deserved to be a national champion.

At the end of the meet, our team finished a disappointing fourth. UCLA won, just one point ahead of LSU. I ended up never winning a team national championship at Texas, but I was ready to take the next step in my track and field career.

SANYA SAYS

Looking at the stat sheet, you'd think I'd want to forget about the 2004 NCAA National Track and Field Championships. Third in the 400-meters. Sixth in the 4x400 relay. Sure, there were disappointments in that meet, but there was one shining moment—when Nichole won the 100-meter high hurdles in record-setting time.

Nichole had worked so hard and deserved the moment. Even though I was disappointed for myself, I was really happy for her.

The Bible tells us, "Rejoice with those who rejoice; mourn with those who mourn" (Romans 12:15). We show God's love by getting the focus off ourselves and being genuinely happy for someone else's success. Share in your friends' or teammates' joy, and remember to be there for them in the hard times too.

Chapter 7

GOING PRO

*"The LORD is my light and my salvation—
whom shall I fear? The LORD is the stronghold
of my life—of whom shall I be afraid?"*

—PSALM 27:1

The summer of 2004 featured the pinnacle of track and field—the Olympics. Track is huge in Jamaica, Europe, and other countries nearly every day of every year. But the whole world watches the Olympics. Making this event even more special, the Games were going back to their birthplace of Athens, Greece.

To earn a place on Team USA, I'd have to run a lot better than I had in Austin at the NCAA championships. The US Olympic Team Trials can be just as competitive as a big international race . . . and even more nerve-wracking. If you don't perform well at the trials, you don't make the team. Plenty of world-class athletes have suffered through one bad day and watched their Olympic dreams be dashed.

With about a month before the trials, I knew I had to renew my focus. Physically, I had been ready to run at the NCAA championships. But I made the mistake of going out too fast in the 400-meters. I was eager and excited. At nineteen, I didn't have the experience of some of the other athletes. But at the trials, I promised myself to have greater patience and run my race. It paid off!

I entered the eight-day meet in Sacramento, California, feeling strong and with something to prove. I breezed through the 400m quarterfinal and semifinal rounds with the fastest time in each heat. In the finals, I ran 49.89—nearly a second faster than the 50.68 I posted in the NCAA championships.

Only the 28-year old veteran Monique Hennagan finished ahead of me to win the trials, but the top three placers
all earned the right to wear the red, white, and blue at the
Olympics. DeeDee Trotter took the final individual spot. As
the fastest runners, the three of us and several other athletes
also qualified to compete in the 4x400 relay.

Of course, I'd hoped to win. But by running under 50 seconds and claiming second, I'd accomplished my goal of making
the team.

All Greek to Me

In the middle of August, more than 10,000 athletes descended
on Greece. It was the best of the best. Walking with Team USA
in the opening ceremony was as close as I'd ever felt to being
in the movies.

Waiting to walk onto the field was the hardest part. Because
our country starts with *U*, most nations get introduced before
the United States. But the wait was worth every minute.

Stepping into the arena was electrifying. Cameras were
everywhere. Music blared. Fireworks exploded overhead. At
that moment, I realized the magnitude of the Olympics and
how fortunate I was to be one of the few athletes that got to
represent her country. I wanted to give everything I had to
make everyone at home proud. And I also hoped to get a little
camera time so my friends at home could see me!

I tried to soak it all in, even taking pictures and talking with my favorite basketball stars LeBron James and Carmelo Anthony, while still remembering why I was there—to win a gold medal.

The track and field events didn't begin until a week after the opening ceremonies. During that wait, I worked out with the rest of Team USA. But I also had some time for fun.

Once the competition began in Olympic Stadium, it was all business. First up for me, the 400-meters. Unlike high school and college meets where I helped the team any way I could by running the 100m or 200m and being part of other relays, my sole focus was the 400m—both individually and as part of the 4x400 relay.

In the individual finals I drew lane 2, right next to the race favorites—Mexico's Ana Guevara and Tonique Williams-Darling of the Bahamas. The battle for the gold ended up being between those two runners with Tonique making a great push in the final 50 meters to win gold. My teammate, Monique Hennagan, was edged out at the tape by a Russian runner for bronze. Monique, DeeDee, and I ended up placing fourth, fifth, and sixth respectively. Had I run my fastest time from that season, I would have earned bronze. Although none of us earned a spot on the podium, our finish showed we'd be a force to be reckoned with in the 4x400 relay.

THE INSIDE TRACK

One of the best parts of the 4x400 relay for an athlete is that you get to watch all the handoffs. In the 4x100 and 4x200 relays, baton exchanges happen at different parts of the track. With the 1,600 relay, all the competitors wait in a big group at the transition zone until it's their turn to run.

Before every relay at the 2004 Olympics, we prayed together as a team, not to win, but that we would all run to our full potential. Once the race started came the best part—standing with your teammates cheering for each other! Some athletes prefer to stay quiet and focused, but for me encouraging my teammates and screaming for them is a part of what makes the relays so special.

Four days later, we proved that fact when Monique Henderson joined our foursome to help us take gold.

One of the great things about the Olympics, and sports in general, is that you can go from rivals to teammates in a matter of months. In June, DeeDee, Monique Henderson, and I had battled for a college championship. Now we were working together for the glory of our country.

As the Olympic final began, DeeDee got us off to a good

start. Only the Russian team was slightly ahead of us by the time Monique Henderson took the baton.

Monique sprinted into the lead right away, opening up a 3-meter gap down the final stretch as she approached me. I grabbed the baton from her and took off. Just like in the open 400-meters, I pushed myself to get up to speed. I couldn't hear anything or feel any other runners around me.

Looking back at recordings of the race, the Russian and Jamaican runners narrowed my 6-meter lead to about 3 meters coming out of the third and fourth turns. But down the homestretch, I had plenty of kick left. I reopened a huge lead and passed the baton to Monique Hennagan knowing we would win. She had helped Team USA win the gold in the 1,600 relay at the 2000 Olympics and was the perfect anchor for our team.

Monique ran a great lap. She was never challenged, and we won the gold medal by more than a second.

As soon as she crossed the line, we gathered in a group to celebrate. For three of us, it was our first Olympic medal, and it was gold! We bowed our heads one more time, thanked God, and took off on our victory lap. With four girls, we stopped around the stadium at least four times to celebrate with family. It was pretty unforgettable.

We were Olympic champions!

Hart of a Coach

After winning gold in the 4x400 relay at the Olympics, I knew I was ready to move beyond the grinding team schedule of college athletics and pursue my potential as one of the world's best. But to do that, I had to turn pro.

I announced my decision to turn professional shortly after the 2004 Summer Games. According to NCAA rules, college athletes can't receive money for running or being sponsored by companies. I signed with Nike, which made me a professional athlete.

Now I needed a coach. Hard work and believing in yourself will only get you so far. The best athletes have wise coaches who speak into their lives, pass on tried-and-true training tips, and keep them focused on their goals.

In Athens, I had watched Jeremy Wariner win the 400-meter gold medal. As a student of the sport, Dad knew Jeremy was coached by Clyde Hart. Coach Hart had also guided world-record holder Michael Johnson to gold medals in the 400-meters at the 1996 and 2000 Summer Games.

Coach Hart was universally respected as *the* master tactician and teacher of the 400. Nobody was better. Of course, I wanted him mentoring my budding career. There was just one problem. He had never coached a world-class woman before.

After talking to Coach Hart over the phone, my dad and I

drove ninety minutes north of Austin on Interstate 35 to meet Coach Hart in Waco, Texas. I think something in me sparked Coach Hart's curiosity. As the longtime track and field coach at Baylor University, maybe he wanted to see if his philosophy in the 400-meters would also apply to a woman.

He told me that my reputation as a hard worker gave him confidence I would thrive in his training environment. We agreed to work together for one year and then re-evaluate the relationship. He ended up guiding me for all thirteen years of my professional career and remains one of my greatest teachers.

SANYA SAYS

At the start of every new season, Coach Hart and I would sit down and go over my goals for the upcoming year. Every meeting would end the same way. He'd look me in the eyes and say, "If you can only get one percent better this season, you will remain the best in the world."

To improve by one percent, took three hundred and twenty-three days of training. All of that sweat, effort, and discipline to shave a couple hundredths of a second off my time. For most people that would be maddening. But picturing myself standing on the top of that podium and realizing a lifelong dream kept me motivated and inspired.

Sometimes it takes a lot of work to see little gains. God rewards obedience. Often it's obedience in the little things that makes the biggest difference.

PACE

Finding Rhythm with God

Chapter 8

UNDER THE WEATHER

"If anyone thinks they are something when they are not, they deceive themselves. Each one should test their own actions. Then they can take pride in themselves alone, without comparing themselves to someone else."

—GALATIANS 6:3–4

From the time I was a child, being a professional athlete was all I ever dreamed of. Once I achieved my goal of being paid to run, finding my rhythm took some time. Juggling schedules, being away from home so much, and competing around the world came with plenty of obstacles. I had to deal with missing my family, not having some of my favorite foods, and running in varying climates and weather conditions to name a few.

When I arrived for finals at the 2005 World Championships in Helsinki, Finland, I really thought race organizers would cancel the competition due to rain. It was coming down in sheets. I could barely see out of the bus windows when we pulled up to the stadium.

But tickets were sold, the stadium was full, and there was a strict schedule to maintain. Officials handed us umbrellas as we stepped off the bus and pointed us to athlete check-in.

On the uphill trek through wind, rain, and thunder, my umbrella buckled and was sucked up into the sky. My hoodie and rain pants were no match for the torrential downpour. Before even checking in, I was soaked from hair to toenails.

This wasn't the way I pictured my second world championships, which was my first where I was ranked as one of the favorites. I walked from the athlete check-in to the track, struggling to keep my mind in the game and not on the weather conditions and my discomfort.

This can't be happening, I thought. *Surely, the organizers know we can't run in this weather.*

Rain covered my oval office in currents of water. I stared down at the track and my soaking socks, totally distracted from my main objective—beating Tonique Williams-Darling.

The powerful runner from the Bahamas had won Olympic gold in the 400-meters in Athens. Since then, she'd posted the top four times in the world in 2005. She was my main competition for the world championship.

Tonique had beaten me at a major track meet in the United States in June. A month later, during the European racing season, I had answered with a win of my own. Tonique didn't have the physique of a typical quarter-miler. Unlike the long, lean legs of typical runners in the event, Tonique's popped with chiseled muscle. Many 400-meter runners look like they're gliding around the track. Tonique didn't glide. She powered her way around the oval.

She announced her presence at the World Championships with a regal aura. She and her entourage arrived for the finals as the rain fell harder and heavier by the minute. With her hair and makeup like a beauty queen, the water seemed to slide right around her. Looking at her, I felt more intimidated than ever.

All Wet

The night before the finals I had a conversation with a runner I really admired.

"If you want to beat Tonique," he said, "you have to beat her off the curve."

I wanted to tell him that when I won in Lausanne—the waterside Swiss city that's home to the International Olympic Committee—I had made up ground on Tonique coming through the turn into the home stretch.

But I didn't have the nerve to say anything. I was young, and he was more accomplished. I believed his advice. I thought if I did something different—something extra—it would guarantee a win.

Back on the track, the rain continued. Coach Hart said it was the first and only time he'd ever seen a track covered in curling waves of water. The last thing Coach told me before I walked out to my lane was, "Push, pace,"—a reminder of our strategy in every race. To win, Coach Hart believed in powering through the first 50 meters with everything I had. Then I'd throttle back to find my rhythm for the last half of the race. If I paced myself through the final turn, I could kick it down the home stretch and fly to the finish line.

It sounded good and it had worked for me in the past, but it wasn't the advice I had been given the night before.

Push, pace, whatever, I said to myself. *I'm beating her off the curve. I'm winning this final.*

I drew lane 3. Tonique had lane 6. Running on the inside of your biggest rival can be, and should be, a big advantage. You can see her pacing and position and don't have to worry about somebody sneaking up from behind. When it comes time to make the final turn, and really race, knowing how your toughest competition is doing can be an asset.

This time, though, Tonique became my target. I was fixated on her, instead of my lane and my strategy. I was intent on beating Tonique around the last curve. I did, but in doing so I neglected the Four Ps.

With rain still falling, I exploded out of the starting blocks. Before I had completed the first turn, I had already passed Olympic silver medalist Ana Guevara. Later, listening to a TV replay, the announcers remarked at my incredibly fast start. I did a better job pacing myself the next 100 meters. Then I

UNDER 50

Running a full lap around the track in under 50 seconds is something few female athletes can claim. Add in race conditions and other pressures, and a sub-50 400-meters is a rare achievement in competition.

Throughout my career, I posted forty-nine sub-50 times, the most in history, in the biggest track meets. I grew up wanting to be like Merlene Ottey, the "Queen of Track," and I eventually earned my own nickname, the "Sub-50 Queen."

pushed too hard through the final curve. I was in front of the pack as we began the homestretch, but my legs were all out of running. All my energy had been used up chasing down Tonique. I couldn't hold the lead.

All I could do was hang on and finish second in the world championships. Ana had run a smart race and nearly caught me at the end to take third.

For a twenty-year-old in her first full season as a professional, earning a silver medal at the World Championships with a time of 49.74 should have felt like an accomplishment. But I was heartbroken. Not because I had lost, but because I beat myself running someone else's race. I had let the voice of another runner clutter my mind, instead of listening to my coach. Coach Hart knew me best and had the best strategy in mind. I was upset because before I ever stepped onto the track and squinted through the downpour, I had talked myself out of winning.

That loss in the 2005 World Championships was one of the hardest things I've had to overcome. The moment I crossed the finish line, I knew I had second-guessed myself to a second-place finish. I hadn't trusted my plan or myself when it mattered.

It was a hard lesson learned, and a mistake I vowed never to make again.

"They can't beat me if I run my best race." Those words

became a slogan that I'd say to myself before every race through-out the rest of my career.

SANYA SAYS

I was humbled after losing the 2005 world title to Tonique. Mostly, I was angry for not believing what I knew in my heart to be true: God had helped make me the fastest 400-meter runner in the world. A few days after the race, I visited with Coach Hart.

"Coach, I'm going to win out," I told him. "I'm going to win the rest of my races this year, and I'm going to be ranked No. 1 in the world."

Usually the world champion earned the *Track and Field News* top ranking. But I knew if I won my final races—if I ran to my potential—I could take the top spot.

Not even two weeks later, I ran a personal best in Zurich, Switzerland. Then I closed out the season with another victory in Monaco. I ended the season ranked No. 1. And my time of 48.9 seconds in Zurich was the fastest 400-meters in the world that year. I also became the youngest woman to ever break 49 seconds.

Yes, Tonique was in both races. But it didn't matter. I had the winning formula inside me all along. I kept my pace, ran my race, and let the results take care of themselves.

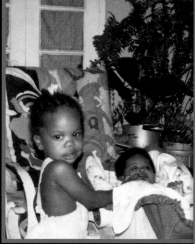

My sister and me

My dad and me as he massages my mom's and sister's feet

Winning the 60-meter race against Vanessa while at Vaz Prep

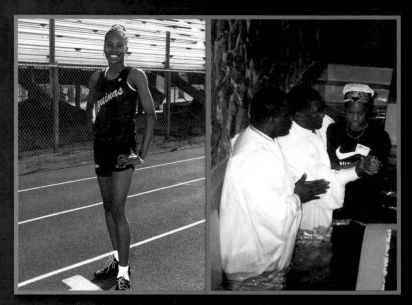

My freshman year at St. Thomas Aquinas

My baptism at age thirteen at ChristWay Baptist Church

Named 2002 Gatorade High School Athlete of the Year

Pep talk from Dad before competing at the Junior
Nationals in Raleigh, North Carolina

Dad's Prefontaine
Classic ticket

Competing at the
Texas Relays

Training session with
Coach Clyde Hart

Supporting Ross after one
of his UT football games

Jamie McDonald/Getty Images

After breaking the American
record in the 400 meters at the
2006 World Cup in Athens

Mark Dadswell/Getty Images

In transition—the 4x400 relay handoff in Osaka, Japan, 2007

Start of the 400-meter race at the 2008 Olympics in Beijing

My disbelief that I blew it

Jeff Siner/Charlotte Observer/MCT via Getty Images

My determination to win for my team at the 2008 Olympics

Fabrice Coffrini/AFP/Getty Images

Gold medal presentation with my 4x400 relay team at the 2008 Olympics

Wedding day, February 26, 2010

Victory in London in the 2012 Olympic Games

Victory lap at the 2012 Olympics

My farewell at the 2016 Olympic
Trials in Eugene, Oregon

Chapter 9

RIGHT ON TIME

*"I lift up my eyes to the mountains—where does my help come from? My help comes from the L*ORD*, the Maker of heaven and earth."*

—PSALM 121:1–2

Coach Hart isn't the type of coach who lines you up to race against your teammates every day. At most practices you run against a buzzer. The buzzer sounds at the exact instant you should be at each 50-meter mark. If you're at a bright orange cone when it sounds, you know you're going to make your time.

It's a great way to help you keep pace and be on time.

When you think about it, time is everything. Being on time, wishing we had more time, and saving time. Our lives are defined by how we spend our time.

On the track, it's the same way. Those little numbers on the clock are big influencers—the difference between good and great, first and last, fast and slow. You have to beat time, but you can't be controlled by it.

Heading into the 2006 season, time started to get the better of me. Instead of being a motivator, it became a distraction. I was always looking at the clock—not the finish line.

Even though I finished 2005 in a flurry and was ranked No. 1 in the world, I was still relatively unknown on the worldwide racing circuit. Everyone was chasing Tonique, the reigning Olympic and world champion.

Mom traveled with me during the European season and also worked as my manager. Coach Hart dropped in for big races, but his responsibilities as a college coach rarely allowed him to get away. And, of course, we were on the phone 24–7 with Dad.

Dad is incredibly wise and knows me in a way that only a father can. He always encouraged me to win big and win young, knowing the window to compete at an elite level is sometimes short. His advice was to break records and win races as early and as often as possible. Like most fathers of great athletes, my dad was committed to helping me become a champion.

With little pressure and no bulls-eye on my back, I made it my goal to beat the American record in the 400-meters. Standing between me and the record was its present holder Valerie Brisco-Hooks, who ran 48.83 in 1984. By August 2005, I was within one percent of that time after running 48.92 in Zurich. So the 2006 season became all about chasing down the American record.

Beat the Clock

Coach structured my training so I'd run two or three early meets, just to get my legs and my mind in race mode. Then by late May or June, we hoped my times would significantly drop as I pulled back the volume and intensity of my training sessions and just focused on racing.

I opened the outdoor season by running a 50-something 400m in Waco, Texas. That dropped to 49.89 at a race in early May. Then I busted out a 49.27 on June 24 in Indianapolis. Coach Hart's plan had me on target. As we went overseas for the Golden League competition, I was ready to go for my goal.

Schedules at international meets were always different. I was traveling with my mom and with my teammates, including Olympic and world champion Jeremy Wariner. Sometimes I'd run first. Other times Jeremy would. Traveling and training so much together, Jeremy and I became friends. We'd discuss our race strategy and make friendly bets about who would have the better performance. Of course we didn't run the same times. At the world-class level, men usually run faster than women, if they've trained hard enough. Coach always measured our performances based on a five second differential. So if I ran 49.2 and Jeremy ran 44.3, my performance was better by one-tenth of a second.

I loved when Jeremy ran first. Then I'd know exactly what time to beat. During many meets I was more concerned about besting him than beating my competition. We were both on undefeated streaks and didn't even notice it. With a different focus, racing became fun again and took a lot of pressure off the actual competition.

My fastest races suddenly felt like my easiest races. I would go out hard, maintain my momentum, and distribute my speed evenly around the track. It was pure sprinting with me running my fastest at the end.

But as I got closer to dropping below 49 seconds, the clock became my enemy—literally. I hadn't realized it, but I'd always look at the clock during the last few meters of a race.

Although I didn't notice, Dad did. He was back home watching my races on fuzzy Internet feeds on his computer. Even with the delay and poor video quality, he was able to track my eyes and how they moved away from the finish line and to the clock during my last few strides.

"Sanya, if you don't look at the clock, you'll run the time," he'd tell me after each race. "The clock is slowing you down."

With my eyes distracted, my mechanics slowed down. The body goes where the eyes go. So while my body was going forward, my eyes had shifted off course. And because I'd learned to anticipate the finish line, sometimes I'd dip my shoulder and lean before the end. Without full extension, I'd lose a little momentum.

These subtle movements might not be discernible to fans. But every detail counts when you're trying to cut the smallest amount of time. Add up the movements, and it's half a second—and that's what separated me from the record.

Record-Breaking Run

The last race of the season was the World Cup, held inside Olympic Stadium in Athens. My fitness was supreme. I held the fastest time in the world at 49.05, but drew lane 7. The World Cup has a funny system—lane assignments have nothing to do with times or rankings. Your country determines your lane. For some reason, Team USA drew lane 7. Being that far out on the track in a staggered start made me the hunted instead of the hunter.

I considered my lane a disadvantage. My competitors could set their pace off mine. I was forced to run blind, not knowing who might be ready to overtake me.

My ever-optimistic father encouraged me to find a different perspective.

"Let it work for you, baby girl," he told me over the phone. "You'll have no distractions."

On a nine-lane track, I would have just two runners in front of me. Dad said to pick them up early and don't look back.

"Okay," I said, still not convinced.

"And promise me you won't look at the clock," he added.

I smiled. "I promise."

I didn't really believe looking at the clock slowed me down much. I was running so well in most of my races that my competition was nowhere near me. I enjoyed staring down the clock, demanding that it stop before 49 seconds.

Dad must've noticed something in my voice. He begged me to try something different. "What do you have to lose?" he said. "You've done it your way all season. Let's try mine."

"Okay, okay," I said, laughing. "I *really* promise."

When Dad made me promise to keep my eyes straight ahead, I felt nervous. Looking at the clock gave me the feeling that I could reach deeper, kick harder, and beat the record. I

FAST TRACK

When I set the American record in the 400-meters, my average speed was 18.7 miles per hour, and I even broke the 20 mph barrier. Track stars are fast, but we're not the speediest of God's creations. Check out this list:

- Usain Bolt is called the fastest man in the world. When he set the world record in the men's 100-meter dash, he reached speeds of more than 27.5 miles per hour.
- Cheetahs are considered the fastest land animal. They've been clocked at around 65 mph.
- Peregrine falcons can dive at the ground going more than 240 mph.
- Sailfish can swim more than 65 mph for short distances.

was focused on winning in my own strength. Dad wanted me to trust more in God's strength. God asks us to run on faith not by sight. By not knowing the time, I had to rely more on my training and on God.

As I settled into the starting blocks for the finals, I told myself one last time: *No clock, all finish line, all faith.*

Bang!

I felt no fatigue as I sprinted out of the blocks. Within 10 seconds, I had passed the runners to my right. The rest of the race was between me and my mind.

I wasn't used to the dimensions of the track in lane 7. I rarely ever ran in that lane, so the turn came more quickly and everything looked different. From lane 4, I know my exact sight lines at 100 meters, 200, and all the way around the track. But in lane 7, I was never sure exactly where I was until I came into the final 100 meters. I was just running free, running from instinct, and running with power.

As I sprinted down the home stretch, I maintained my promise. I stayed relaxed and ran through the line. I knew I'd won, but I didn't know my time. Finally, I looked at the clock: 48.70. A new American record!

I looked into the stands and couldn't find any friendly eyes to connect with. My mom was the only one who made it to Athens, and I had no idea where she was sitting.

Does anybody know what I just accomplished? I thought. *I'm the fastest American to ever run the 400 meters.*

After I left the track and found my mom, we had plenty of time to celebrate. The race that chose me had given me the greatest gift. My name was now etched in the record books alongside US track greats such as Flo Jo, Michael Johnson, and Jackie Joyner-Kersee.

SANYA SAYS

The narrower your focus on the track, the better. Maintaining that focus is just as important at the end of a race as it is in the beginning. For those crucial first 50 meters, I looked as close as I could to my body. My eyes carried maybe 10 yards ahead of me. If I looked around and saw my competition, I could get anxious.

God doesn't want us to look around and compare ourselves to others. We must stay committed to our true path and avoid distractions. Each and every day, we have the opportunity to move closer to fulfilling God's plan for our life.

God can accomplish in a moment what could take us a lifetime. We can't even begin to understand his power. Just like on the track, we need to keep a narrow focus in life. Our gaze should only be pointed in a single direction, to the undefeated Champion of champions.

Chapter 10

TUNNEL VISION

"So whether you eat or drink or whatever
you do, do it all for the glory of God."

—1 CORINTHIANS 10:31

I always dreamed of breaking records. Not just American records, but world records. My goal was to be the best female quarter-miler ever.

But after setting the US record in 2006, the world record seemed nearly impossible.

If you look at most records in track, swimming, or other sports that compete against a clock, times gradually drop. As technology gets better and techniques are refined, performances progressively improve.

In the 1980s, the women's 400-meter record was demolished. An unbelievable three seconds were shaved off in a ten-year span.

For a comparison, look at the men's 400-meter world record. In the course of twenty years, from 1968 to 1988, the record was lowered by less than six tenths of a second. During that time, it went from 43.86 to 43.29. That's a difference of .57 seconds. Compared to that, three full seconds is ridiculous to think about!

Yet in October 1985, East German runner Marita Koch ran 47.6 at a World Cup event in Canberra, Australia. That's more than a full second faster than my American record of 48.7. No woman has come close to running that fast since then.

In fact, no athlete has even run sub-48 since the 1980s. Marie-Jose Perec, a French runner, came the closest when she won her second 400m gold medal at the 1996 Atlanta

Olympics. Her time of 48.25 is an amazing accomplishment in itself.

What Marita Koch did in 1985 simply doesn't happen today. Many experts, however, attribute her performance to the excessive use of steroids during that time.

Marita competed in an era when East Germany was known to systematically "dope" its athletes. In sports, *doping* means to give chemicals or drugs to an athlete to enhance his or her performance. Many of these drugs, such as steroids or human growth hormones, are dangerous to an athlete's health. The chemicals can also have harmful side effects.

In some cases, the athletes never know they're taking drugs. Their coaches or medical professionals give them the chemicals in shakes, shots, or pills. Other times people have purposefully taken drugs to gain an unfair advantage. In either case, doping is illegal.

Many of Marita's East German teammates, who raced with and against her, have since admitted they doped in a state-sponsored program administered by the country's secret police.

In 1990, when East Germany and West Germany became one country again, secret records were made public. These documents detail substances, quantities, and the athletes who received them. Later, a book was published containing doping data for East German athletes that included Marita.

For her part, Marita never failed a drug test. She has also never publicly admitted to doping.

So the women's 400-meter record stands at 47.6, though it remains clouded in suspicion. I believe, and many others agree, it was a record that was created in a lab.

Throughout my career, the recipe for success was never simple. Dad and Mom never allowed me to believe there was a magic pill or secret formula. Everything revolved around commitment and discipline. It wasn't easy. Many times it was painful. I lost plenty of blood, sweat, and tears on the track. But all that hard work made the triumphs that much sweeter.

The reward of standing atop the podium, after doing things the right way, is one of life's best gifts. There's a power in knowing something is pure. The outcome isn't promised. Each day I worked in faith, hoping my effort would pay off.

On Board

Another thing the 2006 season taught me was that if I wanted to achieve a goal, I needed a clear vision and purpose. Because I locked in on breaking the American record, I was able to identify—with help and advice from Dad and Coach—steps where I could improve. With every step, I made progress and eventually accomplished the goal.

I turned that lesson into a tool for the remainder of my career. At the start of each year, I sat down at my dining room

DO AND DIET

My dad, with his Jamaican heritage, believed in eating from the land. He faithfully juiced vegetables and fruits every day to supplement my diet. Growing up, he watched what I ate like a hawk. My family didn't eat pork or red meat. We'd fill our plates with colorful vegetables, fruits, and whole grains.

"We don't cheat," Dad would say. "We use the power of the earth to win."

Then he'd hand me a tall glass of rainbow-colored juice. Containing a bittersweet mixture of spinach, beets, oranges, ginger, and the like, I'd hold my breath and gulp it down.

No steroids for me. My edge came from the goodness of God's creation.

table and constructed a vision board. No small dreams for me. I went big!

At the center of the board, I always put the cross, my constant reminder that all things were made possible through Christ. My greatest desire was to please him. Then I used my creativity to build visual reminders of my goals. I'd cut out pictures from magazines, turn gold foil into gold medals, and write motivational phrases around the border. No dream was too crazy or off limits. This project was an expression of my happiness and eagerness to do the hard work.

By consistently putting together a vision board, I was able to narrow my focus. This practice also challenged me to be clear on what I wanted. What I liked most about the process was that it forced me to dig deep within myself and ask some important questions:

- What has God put me on this earth to accomplish?
- How can I be an example or role model for others?
- Who can I serve or support with my talents and gifts?

My vision board was always on display in my house. It served as a constant reminder, helping me mentally prepare for each day. *What is my plan?* Then at the end of the day, I could reflect: *Did my actions align with my goal? Am I progressing?*

For me, a vision board was very powerful. Not only because of the time and tedious work required to create it, but also because it was a gentle motivator—a way I could push myself to make sure I was giving my very best each new day.

SANYA SAYS

God's vision and dreams for us are too great to be limited to a piece of poster board. But creating a vision board is the simplest way I found to identify and go after God-sized goals and lifelong dreams.

By making a plan for success, you can know how to give your best each day. Some days will feel better, stronger, and easier than others. As long as you give everything you've got each day, you'll stay on pace to make your dreams come true.

Chapter 11

WHAT A TRIP

*"Let your light so shine before others,
that they may see your good deeds and
glorify your Father in heaven."*

—MATTHEW 5:16

After my dominant 2006 season, everything changed. My career really took off. Nike, my sponsor since day one of my professional career, began to feature me prominently in advertising campaigns. With greater fame came more requests for personal appearances and photo shoots.

Calls and letters rolled in every day. As my manager, Mom was overwhelmed just trying to keep up with emails and contractual commitments.

In track and field, the prize money awarded for winning races is modest and only comes in during competition season. In order to make a good living, an athlete needs to get sponsors and make appearances. My mom knew the importance of maximizing my time. We rarely ever declined a request. As a result, my schedule became jam-packed.

I'd juggle weight room work, training on the track, and recovery sessions along with a list of business commitments. I was always on the move. Of course, we had to say no to some requests. One appeal, however, was too good to turn down.

Before the 2007 training cycle began, I was offered $40,000 to make a three-day trip to Japan. It seemed too good to be true. My appearance fees were beginning to approach that number, but this request was not for a competition. My hosts just wanted me to eat at a prominent restaurant, meet with one of their celebrities, and take part in a fun run. From the look of the invitation, it all appeared so simple . . . and fun.

As an athlete, I'd traveled the world for competitions. Even though I'd visited some of the most beautiful cities, I'd rarely had an opportunity to see more than a hotel and the stadium. It was work, and I was always on a mission.

This trip to Japan sounded incredible.

I'd be a guest, not focused on beating the competition, but simply enjoying the experience. Mom and I agreed and soon jetted off in first-class seats to Tokyo, Japan.

Land of the Rising Sun

First up, the restaurant. Just like I'd seen on TV, we took off our shoes and sat on the ground. A huge table spread before us with one of the largest feasts I'd seen outside of Thanksgiving dinner. Cameras rolling, all eyes focused on me, and I didn't recognize a thing on the table.

Already a picky eater, it was hard for me to find meals in America. I didn't eat red meat or pork. Now I stared at octopus and sushi. I did my best. Closing my eyes, I ate what I could. Our hosts were so accommodating and friendly that I didn't want to offend them. I ended up really liking the spicy tuna roll. I never thought I'd like sushi. But when you try new things, it's amazing what you find out about yourself.

Next, meet a celebrity. She didn't speak a word of English. We spoke through a translator, and it was clear she had a kind

MORNING GLORY

No matter where I'm at in the world, I try to start every morning reading God's Word. Even if it's just thirty minutes, I do a little Bible study, focus on stilling my heart, and say my prayers.

It's these moments in the morning that really help set the tone for my day. Many things try to drag us down. Life is filled with distractions that can get us off track. We all need encouragement. I try to share what I meditate on in the morning with my friends and fans on social media, like this post: *Tough times are not meant to break us but renew our faith and strengthen our commitment to leaning on and trusting in God!*

That's something we all need to remember!

and gentle spirit. Our conversation wasn't long, but it was enjoyable.

Now it was time for my final commitment. I was invited to be part of a fun community race, or at least that's what I had understood it to be. Somewhere lost in translation was the fact that this was no *fun* race. It was a serious event in which most of the participants trained for the entire year.

The course stretched for about five miles. Teams of four competed against each other. Each athlete ran a different distance. The most interesting part was that the teams were staggered, based on their anticipated speed. The slowest entrants went off first, while the fastest team was instructed to take off last. The winning team took home $4,000.

I was put on a team with three ladies who were aspiring professional track and field athletes. They had worked hard to prepare for this race, and the prize money meant a lot.

The pressure was on.

I hadn't started training yet for the year, and I was scheduled to run 1,200 meters—three times my normal racing distance! I panicked.

I don't even run this far in practice, I thought. *How am I supposed to run the anchor leg on a team that starts last against men and women who looked forward to this event like it was their Olympics?*

I didn't know how to answer that question, but I did know I was a part of a team. I had to step up.

Again, everything happened under the watchful eye of TV cameras. On a big screen, I saw the race unfolding. My translator filled me in on all the trash talk and interactions. By the time I was up, there was only one man to beat.

I took off a little too fast, full of adrenaline and excitement. People lined the street, waiting to give runners high-fives and cheer them on. Their passion and my competitive spirit drove me forward.

When I rounded the final curve, I thought I was going to faint. My tank was empty. I was ahead, but the gentleman behind me was too close for me to let up. I gave it everything I had and beat him to the finish line.

I had won for my Japanese teammates. They were so excited and grateful. I was so happy that I decided not to take my cut of the prize money. I wanted them to get as much as they could.

After the race my mom couldn't hold it together. When I saw her, she laughed so hard I thought she might faint. Her joy made me laugh too. What had we gotten ourselves into?

The entire experience was awesome. But I was glad to get back on the plane and head home. Flying over the Pacific Ocean, I realized that my position in the sport and on the world stage had changed. People recognized me, expected top times, put pressure on me to perform ... and I wasn't sure I was ready for all the attention.

SANYA SAYS

My climb to become a world-class 400-meter runner was intense and fast. I was twenty-one and held the all-time American record.

I thought the line to success was a direct path. Every step I had taken led me to the next one. But was the pace too fast? Was the bar set too high? I wasn't sure I could reach the next rung on the ladder.

In racing and in life, you can't get pulled away from your original passion. Fancy trips are nice, but any distraction can knock you off course. To keep your pace, you must stay true to your original commitment and, especially, to God's plan.

Chapter 12

FLEE TEMPTATION

"'All this I will give you,' he said, 'if you
will bow down and worship me.'"

—MATTHEW 4:9

Marion Jones was my biggest hero in the sport of track and field.

That was saying a lot. For me, admiration didn't come down to great performances. I admired people because of who they were. Contributors to society, great leaders, humble servants, and avid believers.

"If you don't stand for something, San, you'll fall for anything," Dad always said.

Integrity meant everything. My family made sure I knew that.

Flight of Fancy

As I readied to travel to my first World Indoor Track and Field Championships in 2006, I was starting to feel like a true professional. This was before I broke the American outdoor record in the 400 meters. I knew that would be my personal goal. But at the time, I was just excited to be part of my third US National team.

My excitement level skyrocketed when I got to the airport and saw Trevor Graham in the waiting area by the gate.

Everyone knew the famed coach. He trained Marion Jones, along with many other bright stars. Born in my home country of Jamaica, he was a former sprinter who was known as *the man* when it came to short sprints. As a track nerd, I wanted to pick his brain. I always loved learning from the experts, and I wasn't shy about introducing myself and stirring up a conversation.

Boldly, I went to the counter and changed my seat on our charter flight to Russia. I sat next to Coach Graham and talked to him the entire way. He was intriguing, smart, and friendly. I hung on every word.

"After you're done dominating the 400 meters, let me coach you," Coach Graham said. "I'll make you equally as dominant in the 100-meter sprint. You're the perfect body type, tall and explosive. You're stronger than most short sprinters and not afraid of the work. You'll be bigger than Marion."

"You want me to come work with you?" I said, shocked. "You think I can be better than Marion?"

I always thought I'd run the 400m for a few years, win the Olympic gold, and then go back to the 100- and 200-meter sprints. They were my favorite races growing up, so I had a lot of fond memories dominating at those distances in high school and for most of my young career.

The thought of training with my hero, Marion Jones, and the great Trevor Graham was compelling. *Very* compelling.

The 400 is a tough race, often considered the most difficult of the sprints. But it doesn't receive as much hype or capture people's attention in the media. Everyone knows who's the world's fastest man or fastest woman. It's the person who wins the 100-meters. Nobody really remembers who won the quarter-mile.

If you could win the short sprints, the endorsements and opportunities were endless.

After taking home five medals from the 2000 Summer Olympics, including gold in the 100- and 200-meters, Marion Jones was the face of USA Track and Field. She had all the sponsors, from Nike to American Express. She demanded the highest appearance fees, and she was on the cover of all the magazines.

I was in high school during Marion's drive for five gold medals at the Olympics. That's when she became my role

DRIVE FOR FIVE

Winning one gold medal at an Olympic Games is hard enough. Winning five is unthinkable. But that was Marion Jones' goal heading to Sydney, Australia, for the 2000 Summer Olympics.

Marion was at the top of her game, cruising to victories in the 100- and 200-meter sprints. She faltered only slightly, claiming bronze in the long jump. Then Marion exceled in the relays by winning a gold medal in the 4x400 and taking bronze in the 4x100.

At the time, Marion's five medals were considered one of the greatest feats in the sport.

model. Her smile. Her athleticism. The way she won with grace and hard work. I wanted to be like her.

As soon as we landed in Russia and I got to the hotel, I called Mom and told her about my visit with Trevor. She was less excited than I thought she'd be.

"I don't know about that group, San," she said. "Too many rumors swirling around them all the time."

I'd seen the news stories that aired in 2004 about Coach Graham and Marion being involved in using illegal substances. But the accusations had never been proven. And Marion had always claimed innocence.

"But Mom, he's Marion's coach," I said. "Marion's been running fast since she was a kid. She doesn't use performance-enhancing drugs. She's the best, and I know I can be just like her."

Fallen Star

I had defended Marion in so many trackside debates. I saw myself in her story and her rise to the top. She was a once-in-a-lifetime athlete. In high school, she was the Gatorade Athlete of the Year because of her success on the track. Then she went to the University of North Carolina and won a national championship with the basketball team. She was that good of an athlete. To me, she was a role model.

So I can't even begin to put into words how much it hurt

on October 5, 2007, when Marion appeared behind a podium wearing a black suit and white blouse and admitted to the world she had used performance-enhancing drugs.

Her confession felt personal. She had betrayed me and so many other young girls who looked up to her. I wanted to feel compassion for her, but I was angry.

Angry that she didn't have the courage to say no to drugs. Angry she didn't believe in her own potential and work ethic to bring her success.

I still believe that Marion could have had a remarkable track career, competing in multiple races and winning most of them, without the drugs. It would have shown the world what success actually looks like. It's not a rocket shooting straight up, but a rollercoaster with highs and lows.

But this idea of being perfect, winning every race, and getting all the money proved more tempting to Marion and her team than standing for something.

As a competitor, that kind of cheating is infuriating. Think about how many athletes did it the right way. They trained, planned their nutrition, and devoted their mind and body to the pursuit of victory. And then they were denied success, because Marion was in the field.

For some people, Marion taught them you can't be the best without cheating. Many people believe shortcuts are the quickest path to success. But the real lesson we should take from her is that the medals, the money, and the magazine covers are temporary. They go away.

The old saying is right: "Cheaters never prosper." They get caught. When you live a lie, the truth eventually comes out. And when it does, there are consequences.

Marion went from being a beacon of light to a dark blemish on the sport of track and field. Her drug use was traced all the way back to before the 2000 Olympics. The International Association of Athletics Federations (IAAF) nullified all of Marion's results after September 2000, including her Olympic titles. The International Olympic Committee stripped her of all five medals that she had won in Sydney.

Then in federal court, Marion confessed to lying under oath about taking performance-enhancing drugs and being involved with check fraud. She went to jail.

As disappointed as I was, I admit that Marion became one of my greatest teachers. She taught me the importance of choices. Integrity is more important than fame. I committed to myself and to God that if I ever became a role model for young girls, I'd give them something real and tangible they could hold on to.

I never wanted anyone to have a reason to rip my posters off their wall or strip my medals away.

I truly believe it's because of the people I had around me that I stayed on the straight and narrow—always sticking to high standards. Most people were intimidated by my dad, but they also saw we were an upright family and team who believed in the fundamentals of hard work.

SANYA SAYS

Unfortunately, performance-enhancing drugs are a part of sports. In any profession, people will look for shortcuts and ways to cheat. Sometimes the idea of winning or being the best clouds our judgment. We desire more—more money, more power, and more things. We become fixated on the destination and mesmerized by what we believe will come with each new level of success.

Don't be fooled. There are no shortcuts. The Bible says, "Ill-gotten treasures have no lasting value" (Proverbs 10:2). The true prize, and the prize that lasts, is in the journey and the success gained the right way. The character you develop by following the rules and acting with integrity can never be taken away.

POSITION

The Race Really Begins

Chapter 13

SPRINT QUEEN

*"Do not conform to the pattern of this world, but
be transformed by the renewing of your mind.
Then you will be able to test and approve what
God's will is—his good, pleasing and perfect will."*

—ROMANS 12:2

B efore the 2007 season started, I decided I wanted to be the "Sprint Queen." While I never followed up on my conversation about working with Coach Graham, talking with him reminded me of how much I loved the shorter sprints.

I had dominated the 400-meters. Now I wanted a different challenge.

My goal was to get better in the 100m dash and dominate the 200m and 400m sprints.

Only one American woman had ever won Olympic gold in both the 200- and 400-meters in the same Games. Valerie Brisco-Hooks accomplished this amazing feat at the 1984 Olympics. My coach knew somebody else who had done it: Michael Johnson. Coach Hart trained the world-record setting sprinter for his historic victories at the 1996 Atlanta Games. (Interestingly, France's Marie-Jose Perec also took home gold in the 200m and 400m at the 1996 Olympics.)

If Coach Hart could do it for Michael, I thought, *why not me?*

But if I were being honest with myself, my intentions weren't completely pure. I didn't want to switch my focus from the quarter-mile because I genuinely needed to win other events. I switched focus because the pressure of repeating my performances from the 2006 season seemed overwhelming.

I had been undefeated, set the American record, and was named the world female athlete of the year. My nine races under 50 seconds were more than all other women competing

MAN WITH THE GOLDEN SHOES

While it's true that 400-meter runners don't normally gain world-wide fame, Michael Johnson became the exception to the rule in 1996. The twenty-nine-year-old went to the Summer Olympics in Atlanta and captured the imagination of the world. With custom-designed gold Nike racing spikes, his feet blazed as he set records and won gold medals in the 400m and 200m.

His time of 43.49 in the 400-meters was a new Olympic record. Then he ran a mind-boggling 19.32 to shave .3 seconds off the 200-meter world record! His performance had many people calling him the fastest man alive—a title normally only given to the 100-meter dash champion.

that season combined. My photo graced the cover of the most coveted track and field news magazine.

I'd stretched myself and achieved new levels of excellence. Now I feared being able to repeat that same form. If I went out on a different mission, I couldn't fail.

Well, I was wrong.

Out of Focus

I went into the 2007 season at the top; I finished feeling like I was at the bottom.

At a major meet in Indianapolis in late June, I finished fourth and ran one of my slowest 400-meter times since college.

What? I thought to myself. *I go from winning races by tens of meters to not just losing, but coming in fourth.*

At the time of the season when Coach Hart's cycle kicked in and my times normally started to fall, I slowed down. It was a disaster. Instead of exploding around the track, I was imploding.

Mentally, I wasn't there. I had no focus. I was shifting mindsets between the 100m, 200m, and 400m. Even though there's only a few hundred meters' difference, the races are completely different from a mental and physical standpoint. They require totally different engines and strategies.

I thought by adding to my plate I'd be able to reduce the pressure I felt to succeed. Subtraction by addition. Looking back, it sounds silly. And it was. I wasn't able to meet my same standard of success. I lost my purpose, and I lost my way.

Sometimes it takes a misstep, a botched plan, or a poorly run race to bring everything into focus. The 2007 season did that for me. It brought me back to center and put me back on the correct path.

Isn't that the beauty and power of grace? God gives us the power to stand back up and try again.

SANYA SAYS

One of the most repeated commands in the Bible is: Do not be afraid. God knows it's easy for us to fall into a false sense of fear. We look around and grow afraid that we aren't good enough. We fear that God won't love us. We create an ideal in our minds of what we need to do to be better.

The truth is we don't need to be anything. We just need to accept who we are in God. We're his children. In his eyes, we're already good enough. There's nothing we can do to be *better*. Instead of our own efforts, we must trust in God's power.

God's call will sometimes require us to take a leap. A leap of faith, that is.

As children of God, we all share in the responsibility to be positive, bright stewards of God's grace. That sounds like a simple task. Maybe that's what's scary. While it may be simple, it's not easy. Keeping faith requires a daily focus and commitment. Yet we get lost on the journey by creating other missions and visions for our lives.

In the race of life, we can know our position is always first place in God's eyes.

Chapter 14

GETTING UNDER MY SKIN

*"Humble yourselves, therefore, under God's
mighty hand, that he may lift you up in due time."*

—1 PETER 5:6

A couple things can signify you've made it in sports: huge corporate sponsors and rubbing shoulders with megastars.

Both were happening for me.

AT&T signed me as one of their ambassadors going into the 2008 Olympic Games, and NFL great Deion Sanders was scheduled to come film at my parents' house. Appearing in the 2007 AT&T Home Turf streaming webisodes, featuring some of the country's best athletes, was an awesome opportunity to connect with more fans.

We were all so excited.

It was the biggest production I had been a part of. Tons of emails back and forth, permits to block the streets, trailers, camera crews, producers—the works. I loved being in the spotlight on and off the track.

But about a week prior to the shoot, my mouth filled with frightening white sores that were so uncomfortable I could barely drink water. I went to my doctor, and he prescribed a cream. At the same time, I showed him a wound on my skin that concerned me. He thought the two issues were unrelated and gave me a different lotion for my chest.

At first, the ointments seemed to do the trick. But the night before Deion was scheduled to come to town, the painful mouth ulcers came back. They made it so difficult to open my mouth I wasn't sure if I would be able to talk during the interview.

I broke down and cried. So much preparation had gone into the production that I couldn't imagine letting everyone down.

For an Olympic athlete, sponsorships are few and far between. The Games only come around once every four years, so you have to be ready when opportunities arise. There's pressure to deliver a memorable performance. And you want to be pleasant enough to get the opportunity again in the future.

My mom was so worried. "San, this isn't normal," she said. "We should go to the emergency room."

The pain was bad enough to go, but I wanted to fulfill my commitment. I asked God to clear up my ulcers, if just for a day. Then I'd get back to the doctor as soon as I could.

God answered my prayers. The sores didn't disappear, but the pain was bearable by the time Deion showed up for the shoot. My adrenaline and excitement helped me put on a brave face and a smile. Everything about the day went perfectly, but in the back of my mind I was concerned that this issue may be more serious than I first thought.

Looking for Answers

A week later, the sores were back in full force.

Why didn't the ointment work? I wondered. *What is happening?*

Besides having horrible mouth ulcers, I started having massive lesions on my skin. They started on my chest and legs.

Eventually, they appeared on my arms, back, and stomach. It looked like my skin was poisoned.

As soon as one sore healed, another would appear. The pain from the lesions was overwhelming. But I was used to powering through any pain I faced on the track.

What scared me more was how I would look during my races. To cut down on wind resistance, a sprinter's uniform must be tight and small. It terrified me to have my sores on display for the world to see. I didn't want to have to answer questions about what was wrong with me when I didn't even know myself.

For so long, at a subconscious level, part of my confidence during races came from how I looked. I had grown up being told, "Look good, feel good, run good." I was an athlete who ate well, worked hard, and had a toned body. People always commented on how fit, healthy, and in shape I looked.

Now for the first time, I was terribly insecure about my appearance.

I crisscrossed the country for months looking for a doctor. We visited an infectious diseases doctor in Austin and an ear, nose, and throat specialist in Maryland. I had appointments with almost every kind of doctor there was. But nobody could answer the question of what was happening to my body. What germ or virus was causing me to look and feel like this?

SIGNATURE LOOK

Sometimes God proves how well he knows us by answering prayers before we even ask him.

As I battled the mysterious lesions, Mom and I went to great lengths to cover them and the skin-sagging scars they left. We tried bandages, makeup, anything you could imagine. It was really tough. Then Nike delivered my racing uniform for the season.

I was worried, and so was Mom. But when she opened the package, a smile appeared on her face.

"Look how God works for you," she said.

She pulled newly designed compression arm sleeves out of the box. I couldn't believe it. My arms were affected most. Now I'd be able to cover them in a way that wouldn't seem awkward or forced. After a while, the arm sleeves became my signature look.

Finally, we saw a doctor in New York who said it looked like Behcet's disease, a rare and chronic autoimmune disorder.

No specific tests existed to confirm the disease. My diagnosis was based on the symptoms. But the doctor had an idea of how he could confirm his suspicions. He inserted a clean needle in my forearm and told me if I had a lesion or small red bumps in the area within the next two days, then I had Behcet's.

Two days later I was back in his office. It only took a day

for my skin to explode. I wasn't sure what it meant for me or my career. Behcet's normally affected individuals in Asia and the Middle East. Fewer than 20,000 cases are diagnosis in the United States every year. How had I gotten it? I was so confused.

Amidst my many questions, I was relieved to have a diagnosis and a road map for treatment. My symptoms did not fully disappear. The medication made it manageable at times, but I would suffer with the symptoms for more than seven years.

Coming Clean

As my skin ravaged on the outside, I internally boiled as well. I was scared. I believed that I no longer measured up to the expectations society had for what a strong, athletic woman should look and act like.

Preparing for every appearance was more like a marathon than a sprint. Mom and I strategically picked outfits that covered my ulcerated skin. We tediously applied makeup to camouflage any spots on my arms and legs that were exposed. I was constantly hiding and holding this secret shame. I detested that my body was betraying me.

Then Nike invited me to its headquarters in Oregon to do a photo shoot for its latest product line. Instead of being excited about being the face of a new clothing line, I met this invitation with fear and concern. Around all those cameras, designers, and handlers, there was no way my marked-up skin would go unnoticed. My body would eventually reveal the truth.

Mom and I devised a plan to do our best with cover-up foundation and powder. We arrived on the sprawling Nike campus for the shoot. The set-up was epic. They had pulled out all the stops for this one. Lights and backdrops and people running this way and that.

In the dressing room, I laid my head on Mom's shoulder. She held me in a hug, and I let out a long breath.

"Mom," I said, "I'm tired. I can't hide this anymore."

"I know, baby," she told me. "It's okay."

She gave me the courage to face my fears and admit my private struggles. I walked onto the set and told the truth about my autoimmune disease. It was hard to admit publicly that I wasn't an invincible athlete. But as difficult as it was, it was freeing at the same time. Most people at the shoot were kind enough to not stare. Others couldn't help themselves. But I felt free as I quickly told the room about my condition, smiled, and got to work.

SANYA SAYS

The experience of battling Behcet's disease changed me. I became more compassionate and understanding of the insecurities many women feel every day. I also started noticing more about the messages that advertisers and the media send to girls.

Whether overtly or subliminally, women are often objectified. We're taught to believe that how we look is more important than who we are. That's a lie. The Bible has it right when it says our inner beauty that never fades is more important in God's sight (1 Peter 3:4). Our worth isn't measured by perfect hair or pretty clothes. It's measured by who we are and what we do.

Chapter 15

THE WEIGHT OF GOLD

*"Consider it pure joy, my brothers and sisters,
whenever you face trials of many kinds,
because you know that the testing of your
faith produces perseverance. Let perseverance
finish its work so that you may be mature
and complete, not lacking anything."*

—JAMES 1:2–4

Since my dad first uttered the words when I was nine years old, everything I did was in line with a vision to win the Olympics. I wanted to wear a gold medal and complete the journey from child prodigy to Olympic champion.

Leading into the 2008 Olympics in Beijing, China, I was on a tear. After a disappointing 2007 season, my focus was back. I was training really hard and having fun on the track. I just *knew* this was my time. Nothing could stop me. But something did.

Here's the story of how taking home a bronze medal actually prepared me for the best years of my life. I realized some profound truths about myself and my relationship with God.

The Hard Truth

When I arrived in China for the Olympics, I went on autopilot. I'd worked so hard to get into position to win a gold medal that it became my sole focus. It was all about winning. Nothing else mattered. Tunnel vision is one of the strengths of elite athletes, but it can also have a downside. You can put too much pressure on yourself.

The first day of competition in the 400-meters went well. I won my opening round and posted the fastest time (50.54) out of all the other runners. The semifinal round went equally well. My time of 49.90 was again the best in the field.

But the night before the finals, my mind started working

in overdrive. I'd been pursuing the dream of Olympic gold my whole life. Now it was so close that everything felt like it was going in fast-forward. I couldn't shut off my brain. Shari says I was a babbling fool during dinner. My sister had seen my career as completely as anyone, attending every grade school practice and traveling to most of my college and pro meets.

She was worried about me. She continued to worry all the way back to the hotel where she and Mom were staying. Shari couldn't sleep.

Neither could I.

As I lay in bed, in the early morning hours on August 19, 2008, I couldn't get comfortable. I kept fluffing my pillow, adjusting my sheets. My stomach felt like a big ball of anxiety and nerves.

One o'clock. *I'm wide awake.*

Two o'clock. *My roommate's asleep. Why can't I sleep?*

Following a short, fitful dream, I was fully awake. Looking around the room, I prepared myself for race day, following the routine that had carried me to victory time and time again throughout 2008.

By the time I got to the Bird's Nest, the name for Beijing's amazing Olympic stadium, I already felt fatigued. The night air was hot and muggy—still 90 degrees at 8 o'clock. As a sprinter, you can't feel weighed down. But the heat and humidity pushed me down.

Before the race even started, I was wet with sweat. Coach Hart kept telling me to drink to stay hydrated.

As I walked onto the track, I could feel my confidence diminishing. My sister didn't recognize me when my image appeared on the big screen. Gone were my usual smile, wave, and confident aura.

I got set in the starting blocks in Lane 7 and waited for the starting gun.

Bang!

Finally, I was running. Running for real. I pushed out hard and fast. Within the first 100 meters, I chased down and passed the two runners to my right and was tearing through the first straightaway.

My legs stretched out underneath me. My arms viciously pumped into the next gear. Coming out of the last turn, I was at least three meters ahead of everybody. This was where I usually bounced, where I kicked one last time and flew to the finish. This was where I left everybody behind. They couldn't touch me and wouldn't catch me.

But instead of being clear and focused on executing the 4 Ps, my mind became cluttered. I looked down and saw the Olympic rings on the track. *Poof!* The enormity of the moment hit me. At that same instant, I felt a *pop* in my leg. Doubt began to physically influence my stride.

My right leg jerked stiff and straight. I couldn't shift. Form was gone. Poise was a distant memory. All I could think about was the cramp in my hamstring.

Hold on, hold on, hold on, I kept telling myself.

I couldn't. My dream that seemed so close at hand fell out of reach. The runners on the inside lanes pulled even with me and then surged ahead in the final ten meters. Great Britain's Christine Ohuruogu won the race with a time of 49.62. I was the third one across the finish line at 49.93. I fell to my knees. Even though my hamstring didn't tear, I was broken. My left hand covered my eyes as I tried to bury myself beneath the Bird's Nest.

Grace in Defeat

Somehow I lifted myself off the track. I had entered the race favored to win. Now all I could think was, *It'll be four more years before I have the chance to make my dream come true. At that time, will I still be one of the best?*

As I gathered myself to head to the podium and accept the bronze medal, one of the Chinese officials came toward me with an odd smile on his face. He could tell I was hurting and wanted to say something to change my spirit.

"What happened?" he asked me. "We already had your name on the gold medal."

Trust me, I thought. *I saw my name on the gold medal too.*

The tears burst. A salty, sweaty, uncontrollable flood covered my cheeks.

If the audience could have seen deep within me that day, they would have seen me beaten lower than low. That's how I felt. Eyes swollen by the tears, body aching from the loss, I willed myself to the medal stand. The bronze medal hung around my neck like a symbol of my sorrow.

All I wanted to do was get to my family and the safe harbor of their room. I left the stadium and jumped on a public bus to head away from the media, the village, and my fellow athletes. I needed a refuge, and I needed it fast. Finding a seat, I sunk low. My shoulders collapsed under the weight of disappointment.

Suddenly, a short, violent jolt snapped me into the moment. As the bus lurched forward, I realized that I didn't know where I was.

Was this even the right bus to be on?

I searched the seats for a familiar face—a trace of red, white, and blue; a Team USA hat; anything that looked like home. Nothing. Anxiety began to suffocate me. A full-blown panic attack was setting in.

Weeping, I got off the bus at the next stop. In a city of nearly 12 million people, I felt alone and completely lost.

In the midst of my disappointment, I could only think of a tiny prayer—*Help me, God.* I received an immediate answer. The shaking of my soul began to ease. A sudden peace—a peace that surpassed all understanding—flooded my heart and lifted my spirit. I could hear the familiar, loving voice of my friend, my father, my healer, my protector, my everything, calling out to me that it was okay. I would be okay.

I had failed to achieve a goal that I had worked a lifetime to get, but I wasn't a failure in God's eyes. Until then, I had never truly understood God's love. I knew his love in my head, but I'd never experienced his love deep in my heart. At that moment, I grabbed on to the truth of Isaiah 40:30–31, "Even youths grow tired and weary, and young men stumble and fall; but those who hope in the LORD will renew their strength. They will soar on wings like eagles; they will run and not grow weary, they will walk and not be faint."

I had felt weary on the track and stumbled as I attempted to reach my goal. I thought God would be disappointed in me, because I'd let him down by not using my abilities to win gold. I never hid my faith on the track and wanted to bring glory to his name. I didn't want people to think that Christians were losers . . . that they couldn't perform in the biggest meets.

But in that moment, I realized he was there with me, weeping with and comforting me. He alone could carry me out of my pit of disappointment. He alone could renew my strength and help me soar like an eagle. He loved me the same, even without the gold.

Gentle tears fell down my cheeks as love rushed in.

When I finally made it back to my family, I realized they still loved me the same too. We cried together, but we also laughed. In the midst of any storm, my family could always make me smile. Laughing felt great. King Solomon was right: "A cheerful heart is good medicine" (Proverbs 17:22).

Grace in Victory

Another thing that can heal a broken heart is not giving up and getting back out there. That's what Coach Hart told me.

Four days later, I was scheduled to compete in the 4x400 relay. By this point, God had fully restored my strength and confidence. I understood we are never worthy of the blessings that God bestows on us. His favor and grace are a gift. I don't have to earn God's love; he gives it freely. I stepped on the track freed from the pressures I had put on myself to win.

That freedom showed in my running, because when I took the baton for the anchor leg, Team USA was behind.

The race ended up as a battle between us and Russia. Mary Wineberg started the race for the US. When she passed the baton to Allyson Felix, Russia had a slight lead. Allyson ran a fantastic 400, putting us in the lead. Monique Henderson took the baton next. Russia's runner ran the lap of her life. As I grabbed the baton in the inside lane, we were several strides behind.

It was the first time I had competed in a relay on the world stage and taken the baton *not* being in the lead. Instead of panicking, I stayed patient. Coming off the final turn, I still trailed by about three meters. But in the homestretch it felt like I was floating on air. Instead of falling apart like in the individual 400, I flew past the Russian runner in the final 40 meters and ended up winning by two strides. I had brought my team from behind to win gold!

SANYA SAYS

That 4x400 will forever be one of the most important races of my life. Not because we won gold, but because it was the perfect picture of how God fights for his children. Things may not always happen according to our plan. But no circumstance or experience will keep God from having victory if our hope is in the Lord.

I left China after learning a lot of lessons. I made the Olympic gold medal so important it felt like a mountain of pressure that I couldn't climb. Don't get me wrong. It's important to have goals and work for them. But at the end of the day, He loves us no matter what. That should give us confidence to live every day for him.

Chapter 16

JUST WHAT THE DOCTOR ORDERED

*"But he knows the way that I take; when he
has tested me, I will come forth as gold."*

—JOB 23:10

Track is just a sport."

It was just days after the Olympics in Beijing and the first time I ever heard Mom say those words. For my family, track was our glue. It was our center. But during that time, Mom did what she could to center our family on God.

Losing the gold was a massive loss. Not just on the track but in our hearts.

Even with a broken spirit, I still wanted to run. Running had always been where I felt closest to God. I wanted to do what I knew God created me to do. He made me fast. He gave me a willingness to work.

The track had often been my church, my Bible study, my choir practice. As I walked, jogged, and sprinted around my oval office, I created numerous hymns and prayers that flowed out of my spirit.

One of my favorites is one that my sister and my cousin Yollie still sing with me to this day. It says: *Speak a word, Lord, Deep down in my spirit, Speak a word, Lord.*

I'd sing it over and over as I ran more laps than I could count, begging God to speak to my heart.

My love of track and field started from a place of joy. After more than fifteen years, that feeling had changed. Instead of a place of freedom, the track was at the center of many of my problems. The weight of worry, doubt, fear, and disappointment resided at the track. These feelings were stealing the joy of competing. I needed it to be fun again. I wanted to feel the enjoyment I had had when I lined up as a kid. I wanted running to be pure again.

After I lost in Beijing, Coach Hart urged me to start working with a sports psychologist. I found a doctor and worked with him for about three months. He told me that I put too much pressure on myself to win. He thought it would be a good idea for me to lose a race in order to relinquish the fear of failure when it mattered most.

Throughout my career, I won almost every race of the season. Then I'd go into the biggest race of the year as the heavy favorite, and I'd falter. His idea was to snap my winning streak early and win when it counted.

At some level, I guess it made some sense. Big races, whether it's the Olympics or World Championships, have plenty of pressure of their own. I was probably adding to my load by being the favorite.

During a race early in the 2009 season, I felt primed to win. But I followed my doctor's order and lost. It was the worse feeling in the world.

Why would anyone want to lose on purpose? I thought.

The Right Attitude

I immediately made a change, and it ended up being one of the best decisions of my career. Dr. Don Corley, a Waco-based sports psychologist, became the newest member of my team.

When I explained the strategy my first psychologist had told me to follow, Dr. Corley's expression was priceless.

"You'll never have to worry about that with me," he said. "If you're standing on the starting line, you better believe our goal will always be to win."

THE ROYAL TREATMENT

For my efforts during the 2009 season, I was awarded the IAAF Female Athlete of the Year for the second time in my career. At the awards banquet, Prince Albert of Monaco presented me with the trophy. It was so heavy that I turned right around and handed it back to him.

"Can you hold this while I make my speech?" I asked.

He graciously held the trophy in the background.

When I returned to my seat, my dad was laughing. "Only you would think it's okay to hand the prince your trophy."

Dad loved when I was like that. So happy and light, loving me for just being myself.

It was the start of an amazing, life-long relationship.

He helped me tap into my natural inclinations to focus on the good in every situation, despite the stressors I brought to the track. He taught me to visualize success, seeing every circumstance as a step on the path toward victory.

What I loved most about Dr. Corley was that he was a Christian. Our relationship began to help me achieve my goals on the track, but it quickly evolved into much more. I looked forward to our weekly meetings. His faith steadied me and helped give me a bigger picture of who God really is. We'd talk about upcoming races. Then I'd pick his brain on his faith journey and how he overcame personal struggles. Through his guidance, I further shaped my image of God as a loving, eternal Father.

With Dr. Corley on my team, the 2009 season ended up being a very special year. I went undefeated in six prestigious Golden League races, winning half of the $1 million prize money that was awarded to the athletes who could win all six. I also added nine sub-50-second races to my resume and won my first World Championship title in the 400-meters in Berlin, Germany.

Everything was right—emotionally, spiritually, and physically.

And one of the best parts was that my dad traveled the circuit with me for the first time in my career. He likes to think he was my good luck charm. I know it was the combination of Dr. Corley's support, my dad's presence, and my heavenly Father's unconditional love that made the difference.

It was a memorable season. But the most memorable was yet to come.

SANYA SAYS

One of the things Dr. Corley challenged me to do was explore new opportunities off the track. He taught me that to run the best races of my life, I needed to realize that racing couldn't be my entire life. I had to allow myself to find new projects and follow new passions. If running was all I had, I'd hold it too closely and that wasn't healthy.

But starting something new can be difficult. Many times we allow doubt and fear to knock us off track. Other times doubt can creep in midway through and prevent us from finishing strong. Either way, the most important thing you can do is go for your goals with all your heart, holding God in the center of your vision.

God never takes us where he hasn't already made a way for us. But faith requires action. It's always scary in the beginning, but your faith will increase along the journey.

POISE

Keep Your Eyes on the Prize

Chapter 17

TUNED IN AND TUNED UP

"Let the peace of Christ rule in your
hearts, since as members of one body you
were called to peace. And be thankful."

—COLOSSIANS 3:15

S hari tells me all the time that I have no memory of our life together. Shari is like my dad. They remember everything. Crazy, specific details, like the song that was playing in the University of Texas cafeteria on the day we sat together and I called over my future husband Aaron Ross.

Ross—only strangers call him by his first name—and I were both freshmen. Our careers took off like our courtship. He was a defensive back for the Longhorns with his eyes set on the NFL. Because we were both athletes, I never had to worry about him tempting me with French fries. He even participated with me in my training. Every night when it was time for my sacred 1,000-sit-ups routine, Ross happily joined in and counted for me.

Those are the details that I remember, so I have no idea if Shari's specific memories are right or wrong. I tend to look at the big picture and move forward toward a very specific goal. All the little details don't stick. It's not until someone else brings up a situation, or I see a picture or video, that memories come flooding back.

In spite of this selective memory, I can describe nearly every detail about my significant races. Race days are scripted in my mind's eye almost to the minute. I may not remember the color socks Shari wore to breakfast, but ask me what I was doing six hours before that race, and I'll know. And June 2, 2012, is one of those races I recall vividly.

Peace in the Storm

I was in Eugene, Oregon, for the Prefontaine Classic. It was a Saturday, and I woke up early. My internal clock was still tuned to Texas time, which is two hours ahead of Oregon. I normally got up about nine, so I was wide-awake by 7 a.m.

My hotel room was flooded with bright, peaceful light. Ross couldn't be with me because the NFL always hosts minicamps and other workouts in the summer. I was alone in the room with just my thoughts.

I met my family for breakfast and enjoyed their easy conversation. It was a calm start to the day, which was nice, because from there everything accelerated.

Back in my hotel room, I worked through the visualization strategy Dr. Corley helped me put together, envisioning every facet of the race. I took a short nap to help reboot my mind and body. After about twenty minutes, I jumped in the shower, mostly to rinse off and wake up my body. Then came my favorite part of my race day routine—doing my hair and makeup.

As music from my phone filled the air, I could sense a shift in the atmosphere. Each word felt like rain, dropping promises into my heart and filling me with hope. I sat in front of the mirror, feeling confident and full of expectation. The battle would be real and my makeup represented my warrior face.

I took one last look at the mirror and scanned the room for

anything I may have forgotten. Stepping out of that room, I knew that I wasn't alone. This was God's fight. He was with me.

Headphones on, game face on, I went down the elevator and waited with the other competitors to board the bus to Hayward Field. Letting the music carry me to my quiet place, I felt calm in the storm of race day.

At the track I jogged, stretched, got a massage, and progressed through my drills. Looking into the stands, I saw my dad. I reflected on just how blessed I was to always have him in the trenches fighting with me, believing in my cause.

My dad helped me find my competitive voice. With him by my side, I was able to discover my passion. I didn't just compete to fulfill my dreams and destiny—I was completing his journey as well.

Checking in for my race, I said one more prayer with my family and headed to the call room. Hayward Field was electric with anticipation. As I walked out to lane 4, everything about my day had gone according to plan. Yet despite all my preparation, I started to doubt myself.

The Prefontaine Classic in 2012 felt like a practice for the Olympics, because all the big names were there. Hayward Field was home to both this race and the Olympic Trials, which were set for the last week of June.

I was gripped by questions swirling around in my head. My outlook was growing negative. Instead of reinforcing what

DOWN THE AISLE

In February 2010, my dad walked me down the aisle toward Ross. Ross had fought for and believed in me from the start of my professional running career. We had waited for this moment for a long time. He stood at the altar in an off-white tuxedo, calm and strong as always. His soft-spoken strength was one of the first things that impressed me when we met in 2003. He had the confidence to fill out a football uniform—which he did in two Super Bowl victories with the New York Giants—and the conviction to show his love for his momma. For me that was everything, because family is my everything.

During our long engagement, Ross made it known to me that I was "the one," his only love. We prayed together before every one of my races. Most of the time that was over the phone, because of the distance that separated us. But I never had to worry about another person coming between us in our relationship . . . except for one. God. Knowing God was at the center of our relationship gave me peace. So as I walked toward Ross, secured in my father's arm, it felt right. We had run our race and were crossing the finish line together.

could go right, I was assessing all the things that might go wrong. Looking back, it's interesting that when I felt most

invincible, the Lord allowed me to experience my own human-
ity and weakness.

And to top it off, wind began gusting into the stadium. I
actually chuckled to myself as the weather started to resemble
my inward struggle.

This can't be happening, I thought as I searched for something that was going my way. *Well, at least I braided my hair, so
it won't get in my eyes.*

Thinking of my hair reminded me of a lesson from Luke
12—God numbers the very hairs on our heads. God knows
everything about us. God knows *everything*. So why fear?

Taking a deep breath and closing my eyes, I realized that
my hair was a point to be thankful for. With the confidence
of a daughter whose father was truly watching, I whispered,
"Peace. Be still."

It was more of a cry than a command. A wish to lighten
my load. From Sunday school, I knew Jesus had spoken those
words to calm the storm in Mark 4. When I spoke those words,
I hoped to have power over my thoughts, which were clouding
my goals.

What happened instead was greater than I could have ever
imagined.

The winds in the stadium ceased. God heard my cries and
quieted my storms.

Fight to the Finish

Kneeling down, I settled into my blocks. No matter the outcome, I knew Jesus was running with me.

He was always with me—win or lose.

My racing season had started in the dead of winter with a full indoor schedule. Heading into March, I won my first ever World Indoor championship in Istanbul, Turkey. Running indoors is different because the track is shorter and the corners are banked. But the victory gave me confidence going into the outdoor season.

My first big outdoor race was the Jamaica Invitational at National Stadium in Kingston. Going home always motivated me to run my best. Plus, I was full of fire coming off my World Indoor championship.

I felt confident, but confidence requires balance. It's a razor thin line where pride meets humility. Before many of my races, these two seemed to always faceoff. Even with the right amount of confidence, it's nearly impossible to win every race competing against the world's best. Jamaican Novlene Williams-Mills ran 49.9, a very fast race for early May, and nipped me at the line to win.

Standing in lane 4 at Hayward Field two weeks later, with Novlene in lane 5, had me questioning my form and strategy. Her presence made it difficult to silence the chatter that attempted to drown out what I knew to be true. I could win this race.

Amantle Montsho had earned lane 3. Both Amantle and Novlene are very aggressive runners. After the first 100 meters, they both usually like to hit the gas. Compared to them, I'm conservative on the backstretch. But that means I have to trust that I have enough fuel in my tank to stay poised and kick hard the last 100 meters.

Bang!

The race started and went exactly how I'd thought. When we came out of the last turn, Amantle was a few meters out front. Novlene and I were dead even.

Don't panic, I said to myself.

It was like I inhaled an extra breath. My muscles weren't tense. I wasn't overthinking. I was running free—free of doubt. I pumped my arms to generate a last kick and pulled away.

As I crossed the line, I punched the air with my right arm. The fight was over, and I had won. It was an important win on a big stage.

Within seconds a new feeling washed over me. I started shaking my fists in front of me like a giddy little kid.

This is what it feels like, I thought to myself, *to run with God.* I thanked him for showing me the way to victory and sharing the moment with me.

SANYA SAYS

Athletes are driven by the idea of controlling our outcomes. Since we can't control our competitors or the weather, we become hyper focused on what we can control. The small things become really important on race day: what we eat for breakfast, how long we stay in the shower, when we put on our uniform.

When I came through the final turn at the Prefontaine, I was trailing. But I wasn't afraid. I knew I couldn't control the outcome of the race. I just continued to trust the strategy of my coaches, knowing the Lord was also working with me.

And he isn't about to abandon his work . . . in me or in you.

Chapter 18

VICTORY LAP

"We know and rely on the love God has for us. God is love. Whoever lives in love lives in God, and God in them."

—1 JOHN 4:16

Some victory laps are in the shape of a track oval. Others look more like a figure eight.

I've experienced both.

The minute I stepped into the athletes' village at the 2012 London Games, I *was* the Olympic champion. At least, I was in my mind. I walked and talked as if I had already won. I kept repeating to myself, *I am the champ.*

In preparation for my third Olympics, Dr. Corley had encouraged me to picture every part of the race, including me crossing the finish line first. God gave us powerful minds. The way our bodies function is often directly related to our mental state.

In the past, I'd let negative thoughts and feelings affect my performance. This time Dr. Corley told me to see myself winning. I even knew what I would do when I crossed the finish line. Now I just needed to execute the plan that I had rehearsed hundreds of times in my mind.

The 400-meter final fell on a Sunday. I woke up that morning rested and surrounded by my family. I chose to stay with them in their rented London townhouse instead of at the Olympic village. Honestly, I don't think Shari would have allowed me to do it any other way. She was still scarred from my sleepless, erratic behavior in Beijing.

More than thirty family members and friends had traveled across the Atlantic to watch the race. I appreciated everybody being there, but could only see so many people before the race. My family protected me and charged my spirits. They gave me confidence.

After breakfast, Pastor Gaylon Clark, who led my church in Austin, came by our townhouse. What started as a normal conversation with me and my family grew into a devotional. It was perhaps the only part of the London experience I didn't plan in advance. Pastor Clark reminded me that I was running in the race of my life, but it wasn't on the track. My gold medal was in heaven. I felt God moving in that room. On the couch with Ross, Mom, Dad, my sister, and my aunt, I let the tears flow.

Pulling myself together, I dressed and readied my hair and makeup. As I climbed on the bus headed to London Stadium, Shari turned to Ross and my parents.

"This is it," she said. "This is definitely it."

First, Finally

Everything goes a little slower at the Olympics. Because TV dictates the timing, all the athletes are called to the ready room almost an hour before the race starts. Then we all just jog around, trying to keep our muscles warm and our focus locked in on the race.

I quietly thought through my strategy and anticipated what to expect on the track. Coach Hart's last reminder kept going through my head. He told me the Russian runner to my inside lane starts races like a mad woman.

"She's going to come up on you and pass you," he said. "That's okay. Let her go. She won't be able to hold it."

Finally, we checked in and got our hip numbers. Mine weren't sticking to my uniform because it was so hot.

Oh no, I thought. *Heat.*

I drifted back to my loss in Beijing. *You've run in heat like this hundreds of times.* That internal reminder slapped that negative thought out of my mind.

On the track, I checked everything out in lane 6. When the camera panned on me, I made sure to smile and blow a kiss to the camera.

When the camera moved on, I kept fumbling with my hip numbers, trying to smack them into sticking despite the hot temperatures. I was in my own little world, until the stadium erupted at the announcement of Christine Ohuruogu. The British runner was the defending Olympic champion. Her native country's support was loud and demonstrative. I wasn't anticipating that.

Okay, San, just relax, I told myself. *Breathe. Get back in your zone.*

I didn't plan for the crowd noise, but Dr. Corley and I did plan for distraction. We determined to use it as a source of motivation. As my breathing slowed down and the crowd got

IN THE BLINK OF AN EYE

It takes about one-tenth of a second to blink your eye.

When I won the gold medal in the 400-meters at the London Olympics, I crossed the line in 49.55. Christine Ohuruogu finished with a time of 49.70. That's one-quarter of a second difference—two blinks of an eye.

A lot can happen in a quarter of a second:

- a hummingbird flaps its wings four times.
- the International Space Station flies 1.25 miles.
- 190,000 gallons of water flows over Niagara Falls.

more pumped up, I used their energy to help fuel the intensity of the moment.

One thing I love about the Olympics is that when you get into the blocks, it's like the whole stadium goes with you. Everyone is silent and focused. And then . . . *Bang!*

The gun goes off.

"LET'S GO SANYA!" Shari's voice rose above the crowd.

I charged out hard and found a comfortable pace. About 200 meters into the race, the blonde Russian runner passed me on the left.

That's a good thing, I told myself. *Just like Coach Hart said.*

At the top of the last turn, all I could think was *position*,

position, position. I didn't want to use too much gas and then lose it at the end. Into the last straightway, I felt American DeeDee Trotter next to me. She pulled ahead.

No way, I thought. *She is not beating me.*

I worked my arms, and asked my legs for one more kick. That gave me enough to get in front of DeeDee.

Hold on, just hold on and get to the line, I thought. *Keep your eyes on the line.*

I dipped my left shoulder, punched my right arm through the invisible line, and prayed. That was it. In one of the biggest races of my life, I'd trusted the 4 Ps (and even the fifth P) to perfection.

And I was the champ.

SANYA SAYS

We all have the power to move mountains in our lives. It starts with our belief in a Savior. The Bible says if we have faith the size of a mustard seed we can accomplish great things. Yet many of us lack the faith to lean on God and courageously trust him.

I struggled with this throughout my career. I had to accept my powerlessness to certain forces, giving myself over to trust God to direct my path. At times, it was scary. Following God's will for my life didn't ensure that I would never face hard times or never lose a race.

In fact, the opposite was promised—that I would face trials. But I found strength in believing that God's plan was far better than anything I could dream of. I found freedom in that obedience. It didn't relieve me from the daily work, and the struggle and sacrifice of training. But I was freed from the worry of not measuring up, not being good enough. By trusting God for the result, I silenced the "what if's" in my life.

Chapter 19

KEEPING ON MY TOES

"But if we hope for what we do not yet have, we wait for it patiently."

—ROMANS 8:25

One toe. One tiny toe. Actually, my right *big* toe. But in comparison to the rest of my body, my big toe is small. Just don't tell that to my toe. Its feelings might get hurt.

My right big toe first started talking to me during my junior year of high school.

"Slow down," it said. And I almost cried out. The pain was intense. I told the toe to be quiet. I reminded it that I called upon other bigger bones, muscles, and tendons to motor around a track. I kept running. We had a contentious relationship from that moment on.

Since I was seven years old, I've asked a lot of that toe. It's the toe I coiled my whole bodyweight on top of and pressed into as I begin the push phase of my race. Thousands of times, probably hundreds of thousands of times, those itty-bitty bones absorbed the tremendous force of my running and projected me forward.

My toe eventually broke. I don't remember exactly when—shocking, I know. But the when doesn't matter as much as the why. I worked it, worked it, and worked it some more. The toe didn't splinter or shatter. It just cracked a little to prove a point.

"You're not invincible, Sanya," it told me. "You won't last forever."

I didn't need an X-ray to see the crack. I could feel it. The thunderbolt that shot up through my foot and leg every time I put weight on my toe told me everything I needed to know.

By the time I won the gold medal at the 2012 Olympics, I couldn't ignore my toe any longer. From 2009 to 2012, I was consistently in the doctor's office because of the pain. So when I found a doctor in New York who said he could do a surgery that would shave down a bone spur, create a little more space, and fix the pain, I decided to go for it.

I thought the surgery would extend my career another four years. If I had had any inclination that it would get worse, I would've tried to grin and bear it for as long as my toe would hold up. As an athlete, pain was my training partner. I embraced pain. It told me I was alive and working hard. Every time I hurt, I'd tell myself, *If this is hurting me, it must be killing my competitors.*

So I had surgery on my toe in late 2012. After a couple of months of rehabilitation, I expected to start training again in February 2013. That would give me a late start, but coming off an Olympic year, I didn't mind missing the indoor season. I'd be ready to go by summer, when the European Diamond League races were in full swing.

My toe had other ideas. Following the surgery, my foot became rigid. I couldn't bend my toe and push off to power my stride. I couldn't even put any weight on my toe without feeling pain. It was worse than before.

Training was abbreviated at best. When I'm in season, it's a five-day-a-week job. From morning to night, I'm in the weight room, rehabbing, going through recovery, and then track work in the evening. But the pain and lack of flexibility in my toe made it difficult to walk . . . let alone run.

Still, I always believed in my ability to compete through the pain and run when it mattered. Against Coach Hart's recommendation, I ran at the USATF National Championships in June 2013. The pain was so severe that I sprinted the finals of the 400m in my sneakers. I finished sixth with a time of 51.9 seconds. But everyone joked that I probably set the world-record for running from lane 2 in sneakers.

I decided on another surgery to smooth down the bones. Hopefully, this procedure could help me step more naturally, I reasoned. It was the best course of action, but it also meant I'd be out of work for the summer.

Without a racing schedule to focus on, I had time to consider other passions and talents as a way for me to contribute to the world in a new way. For the first time in my life, I had to imagine life outside of my oval office.

Exchange Zone

For me, the prettiest track and field events to watch are the relays. Four runners blend their talents to compete in unison. A successful relay is not only a harmony of speed, but also a rhythm of reaction.

The baton must be handed off correctly. As runners, we

are always looking for the perfect exchange. It's a rare thing. Numerous times in the Olympics a highly favored team has lost because of a botched exchange. Sometimes, like when the United States 4x100 men's team was disqualified at the 2016 Olympics, a handoff occurs outside the exchange zone. Timing is critical.

I wanted to make sure my timing was right. In life, a lot of what happens comes down to timing. I'd seen it in my own life and in my family's.

A GOOD BOOK

Reading has been a huge part of my life. I can't remember many of the books that I read as a child, but through my career books have inspired me and helped settle my nerves. I've been blessed to travel the world, but I've visited so many other places and met so many interesting people through the pages of books.

By reading, I've been able to step out of my experience and step into the shoes of someone else, gaining an understanding of their world. That's such a valuable experience and has helped me have sympathy and empathy for people in situations very different from mine.

My go-to book was the Bible, which always challenged me spiritually and showed me how to become more like Jesus. So read more, and be inspired!

When I decided to leave college early and turn professional, Shari was inspired to do the same. She had enrolled at the University of Texas to be a computer programmer. But in those classes of 400 people, learning new coding languages, Shari felt lost. She knew what she really wanted to be doing, and it didn't involve keyboards or codes.

Shari was always interested in helping other people look their best. She hid in her closet when we were little, cutting and braiding her dolls' hair. She knew that cosmetology was her life call. When she told our parents she wanted to leave college and go to cosmetology school, they protested. Eventually, my parents agreed when they saw it was her true passion.

In 2009, after Shari finished cosmetology school and built her client base, we decided to open a salon together. It was my first foray into the world of business. And it was perfect for me to have my sister as my first business partner.

The same support Shari gave me on the track, I tried to give back to her as we opened the salon. The timing felt right.

In 2013, my toe was also trying to teach me something else about timing. As much as I wanted to force my toe to submit to my will, it never did. It was time to mentally and spiritually prepare myself for what was next.

Not every blessing is meant to last a lifetime, but hopefully those blessings can propel you forward.

Often we want to hold on tightly and stay in our comfort

zones. But it's when we step out of our comfort zones and trust our successes to God that we realize just how big our Father's plans are for us.

SANYA SAYS

For me, the deep appeal of the relay is how it relates to our lives. Not everybody will understand what it's like to run 100 meters in 10 seconds, but everyone encounters transition. At some point, everyone goes through the exchange zone.

To be ready to jump when the window opens requires self-awareness. You have to know your position, understand where you are, and have a vision for where you need to go. If you're too hesitant to make the move, you may fumble the baton. If you're too jumpy, you may leave too early and be disqualified. You have to commit to God's path and just go when the timing is right.

Chapter 20

NEXT STEPS

*"Trust in the LORD with all your heart
and lean not on your own understanding;
in all your ways submit to him, and he
will make your paths straight."*

—PROVERBS 3:5–6

When I announced my retirement at the start of the 2016 season, I felt a little lost. In my heart I knew it was time, but it was hard to actually do it. I prepared my announcement two weeks prior to actually making it public. I still wasn't sure that I was ready.

But my big toe was sure. It wouldn't allow me to run anymore. I finally came to the realization that I would be passing through a new exchange zone, one that took me off the track but not off track, and it was time for me to accept it.

Once I posted my intentions to retire on social media, I received a flood of support. Past teammates and competitors contacted me personally, gave interviews about me, or replied through their social media that they'd respected me over the years and would miss me on the track.

It was emotional reading their words and hearing their encouragement. These were athletes I admired. To have them wishing me well lifted my spirits and helped me get ready for my last season of running.

The toughest thing about this next phase was that it moved me into completely unfamiliar territory. My entire life had been shaped around winning races. I never had a part-time job, never pursued summer internships, never even considered what kind of career I'd have if I wasn't a professional athlete.

The good news was by performing at a world-class level for so many years, I had access to an impressive network of people.

I knew marketing executives, business moguls, TV and record producers, and numerous top professionals in their fields. They saw the opportunity for me to create my own brand. I just had to open my heart to where God was leading me.

In the build-up to the Beijing Olympics in 2008, I had started down this path, but only superficially. I thought I would win the gold medal and my public image would explode. Obviously, the outcome in those Olympics led me down a different path. But through that experience I realized that although I had a vision for success, I had no clear plan on how to get there.

Creating my own brand required a lot of hard work. I met Kevin Liles, the former president of Def Jam Recordings. He challenged me to articulate what I stood for.

I left that meeting with a lot of questions to answer.

- *What personal pillars had I built my life on that others could connect to?*
- *When people saw me, what did they see?*
- *Did my actions and activities truly reflect the passions of my heart?*

I wanted to leave my career the way I found it, with a passion for excellence and striving to be my best. Following my second surgery in 2013, my right toe had gone silent for a little while. It gave me more time as a full-time professional track athlete. For that, I was grateful.

SANYA'S GLAM & GOLD

When people meet my family, they're fascinated by our bond. Sure, we have conflicts and issues, but we always overcome them with integrity, love, humor, and tons of *patois*, Jamaica's broken English. Hearing people's reactions made me think about creating a family reality show. I thought we had all the components for a hit television series.

I had married my prince charming. My sister and I had opened our own hair salon. Mom and Dad were quite the characters, acting as my parents and managers. And my cousin Yollie was doing all my media outreach and styling.

I plotted out storylines from our real lives. What started as some doodling in a notebook grew into a forty-slide PowerPoint presentation. As a family, we were always a team, with me representing everybody on the field. This would be different. On the show, we'd all stand together in front of the camera.

But the reality of reality TV wasn't what I expected. For one, it's not a fast process. From concept to development, it took about four years. I went from boardroom to boardroom, presenting the concept to talent agents for different networks.

Then when we finally got the green light from WE TV, it took about nine months to begin filming. By the time crews started following us around, the storylines I had presented were distant memories. It was hard to go back and deliver on events that were no longer our reality.

The show, "Sanya's Glam & Gold," aired in 2013. There were glimmers of our real personalities, but we never got a chance to fully be ourselves. The final product was disappointing, and the show wasn't renewed for a second season. The experience wasn't wasted, however, because I learned a lot that I would take into future television opportunities.

Running Out of Time

In 2014, I saw glimpses that anything was still possible. With my toe cooperating, my training became intense. Coach Hart pulled out old notebooks and saw that my times were consistent with those I posted in 2009, when I had won the world championship.

Seeing those results gave me confidence and boosted my training. I finished second at the US National Outdoor championships. Then I won in Paris and Belgium to close out the Diamond League schedule. I was invigorated for what was ahead in 2015.

My offseason from the track wasn't a true "off" period any longer. I knew I had to prepare for the next phase of my life. I made decisions to continue building my brand. Many times there was no pay, just the pursuit of an opportunity. It was tiresome at times, because I was juggling two selves—Sanya, the defending Olympic champion and Sanya, the fashionista, entrepreneur, philanthropist, and aspiring media personality.

Some days I yearned for the innocence I had during my time at Vaz Prep. Back then I was excited by the discovery of new talents and the process of developing them. I didn't have to make decisions. My worries were few. I had only the joy of work.

Other times I realized the new opportunities were no different than my initial discovery of childhood talents. But instead of running around a track, my journey would take me to new places and help me meet new people.

It would be a bit scary. It would be work. But if there's anything my dad taught me, it's that to work is to be blessed.

SANYA SAYS

Persistence is what gets you through the transitions in life. Even when you're not sure exactly what's next, if you push through the exchange zone, God will show you the way. Runners practice handoffs dozens of time before they ever line up for the relay. It's more of an art than a science. No two handoffs are alike. Each one feels a little different. But you always want the same outcome—to pass the baton and keep running. Just taking a step is an act of hope. And the Bible tells us, "There is surely a future hope for you, and your hope will not be cut off" (Proverbs 23:18).

Chapter 21

FINAL LAP

"For physical training is of some value, but godliness has value for all things, holding promise for both the present life and the life to come."

—1 TIMOTHY 4:8

When I arrived in Eugene, Oregon, for the 2016 Olympic Trials, I knew it would be my final time running at historic Hayward Field. Some of my proudest professional moments happened there, and it felt right that I would compete to represent Team USA for a fourth time at the Olympics on this track.

Since winning my first individual gold medal at the 2012 London Olympics, injuries had slowed me down. First, I had to deal with all the pain and procedures associated with my big toe. Then just weeks before the trials, I pulled my hamstring in a tune-up meet.

I had barely run in the days leading up to the trials. I hadn't tried sprinting at all. Part of me knew my heart was making promises that my body couldn't deliver on. But my entire career had been built on my ability to look forward, to keep my eyes up, and to be hopeful in the pursuit of my dreams.

When we finished the workout the day before my first qualifying heat, Dad was by my side. I looked at him in the twilight and thought how perfect everything was. Dad was my ace, my go-to, my steady. I was thirty-one now. We'd begun this journey when I was seven.

"Let's take a walk," I said.

We walked the oval. He pointed out specific parts of the track and what he remembered about them. Normally, we'd go over race strategy and visualize how I would run. This time

Dad and I talked about how far we'd come and what a blessing it was to be here.

"I'm proud of you," he said. "I've always been proud of you."

Walk to Remember

The day of my final race, I was optimistic. I was excited. I also realized I was taking a big chance. My hamstring hadn't had the full six weeks of rest and rehabilitation that it required to truly heal.

I knew I could be setting myself up to fail. But I saw this race as an opportunity for my greatest comeback.

Like he did for all of my races, Coach Hart scribbled the timeline of our warm-up routine on a tiny sheet of paper. Every drill was scripted to the minute. Even though I had every 15-minute increment memorized, I still found comfort in seeing his handwriting.

I struggled to get through my warm-ups. I had the power to burst, but not the strength to shift to the next level. Coach Hart watched me fight against my body and told me it might not be a good idea to run.

"Coach," I said, "I didn't come all this way not to try."

The race started like every race of my life. The gun went off, and I pushed out of the blocks. I charged out as hard as I could, but when I got to the backstretch, I knew I was running a different race. My stride couldn't open, my legs refused to stretch out underneath me. When it was time to make the turn and really go, I had nothing. The field moved away from me, and I couldn't chase them.

When everything in my being wanted to push forward and fly down the homestretch of the track one more time, I just couldn't.

Sanya, be still.

I didn't hear a voice. But I felt those words to my core. And I stopped running.

The first time I raced at Hayward Field, as a teenager, I finished second and the announcer encouraged me to take a half victory lap so the fans could keep cheering me. The track crowd had welcomed me and encouraged my progress. In the thirteen years following that moment, I worked earnestly to fulfill that promise.

As I stood on the track on July 1, 2016, every other runner had finished the race. I was the aging champion. America's next promising talent had run just a few lanes to my right. Courtney Okolo had completed a championship career at the University of Texas, where she broke most of my 400 records.

For a moment, I hung my head.

This isn't the way it's supposed to end, I thought.

Then I heard a voice. A woman's voice, high in the stands. "We love you, Sanya," she called.

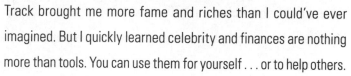

NEW FOCUS

Track brought me more fame and riches than I could've ever imagined. But I quickly learned celebrity and finances are nothing more than tools. You can use them for yourself . . . or to help others.

Serving others is one way I get the focus off myself. I started a foundation, the Gold Standard, to help other athletes get financial support for their dreams as well as support the community through sports and educational programs. And in 2007, I created the Sanya Richards Fast Track program. Growing up, I had received a wonderful education in Jamaica. But I knew that wasn't the case for all students. My program fought illiteracy by helping kids learn to read at their grade level. During the first year, we worked with seventy students in my home country. By 2010, a US-based nonprofit group donated $250,000 to the project, which helped it expand to ten schools and thousands of students.

To me, one of the coolest parts of US Aid giving all that money was this organization saw me as an American citizen doing work in another country. If my mom hadn't gone through the effort of becoming a citizen, the amazing work I was able to do in Jamaica may not have been possible. Competing for the US hadn't been an easy decision and it had caused a lot of hurt feelings, but God turned it into something good. I believe this was part of his plan all along.

It snapped me back into the moment. I lifted up my eyes and started walking toward the finish line.

And would you believe it? The fans stood and cheered. It felt just like when they called my name as the Champion Girl—maybe better.

I knew all the heart and sacrifice I committed to my track career. And the crowd knew it too. They applauded years of dedication and determination. To be recognized for my legacy, instead of my result, lifted my spirit.

I started into a jog, waving to the crowd and blowing them kisses.

I didn't think this was the way my track career would end, but maybe it was the perfect ending.

I had dreamed of something different. I imagined myself circling the Olympic Stadium in Rio de Janeiro, Brazil, with an American flag draped over my shoulders as I celebrated a second gold medal in the 400-meters. I'd take that final lap and walk off into the sunset of legendary retirement.

That would be the perfect ending, I thought.

But we're imperfect people living in an imperfect world. Our only glimpse of perfection comes by focusing on the perfect Champion, God.

My time on the track was finished, but God was just getting started. It was the beginning—not the end. Defeat had lost its power.

The desire to win had me running in circles for most of my life. But as I searched for answers and chased my self-worth in gold, I ran right smack into grace. Now I was stepping out of my oval office, but I knew this wouldn't be my last lap.

SANYA SAYS

When the time came for my biggest transition, the one that would take me away from the comforts of my routine and the glory that came with winning, the change wasn't easy. Yet within a week, a new adventure in broadcasting began. I ended up at the 2016 Olympics, not on the track, but in an announcer's booth. We rarely know what God has planned, but we can trust that his plans are good.

The beauty of grace is that we don't have to be perfect. Don't be discouraged if you don't know what to do. That's the perfect time to put your trust in God, who knows exactly what you need and has the strength to carry you to the finish.

ACKNOWLEDGMENTS

When I began to write this book, I decided on my last chapter first. I knew I wanted to end with a victory lap.

The sport of track and field is unique, because it encourages athletes to take a moment and acknowledge the crowd after achieving a lifelong goal or dream. Few feelings in life measure up to slowly making your way around the track, soaking up the applause and appreciating the crowd for sharing this moment with you.

My victory lap at the 2012 Olympics is one of the most vivid memories of my life. All the friends and family who traveled to London were there in the stadium. As I made my way around, I stopped, took photos, and appreciated each face. I was able to share the peak of my athletic career with the people who stuck by me and supported me along the way. I was grateful to have individual moments with each of them.

I also have so many of them to thank for this book. With faded memories of my past it was most enjoyable to sit with my husband, parents, sister, and cousins to reflect on this amazing journey.

God

Thank you for the amazing gift of speed. I can't believe all the places it has taken me! My hope is that during my career I've been a light on the track, inspiring others.

Now I hope, through the pages of *Run With Me*, I can share your good news in new ways.

Thanks for being the best thing in my life and I pray that you are the same for everyone that reads *Run With Me*.

Family & Loved Ones

Hubby: You are the greatest image of love and humility I have in my life. You teach me every day how to be a better person. You bring out the best in me. Thank you for always being in my corner, for praying with me and believing in this project. I stand tall because you prop me up. I love you ... always and forever!

Dad: You're always there! It doesn't matter if the call comes at 1:00 am or practice at 9:00 pm. You're always ready and eager to help me fulfill my passions. No process feels complete without your stamp of approval or your encouraging words. Thanks for your willingness to help me make this book a reality.

Mom: Thanks for reading every page with me, for jogging

my memory and providing the supplements that no one else could! You have an ear and a heart that knows no bounds. This book is everything I wanted because of your guidance. I love you!

Shari: Even with your newborn son you made time to listen to all my chapter ideas and attend my family book review sessions. You always make time for me and make space in your heart for my dreams. I love you and appreciate you more than you know.

Jesse: You are amazing! It has been absolutely incredible to work on *Run With Me* with you. Your thoroughness, patience, and attention to detail made this book everything I hoped for. I'm so proud of our work together. Thank you so much!

My Team: To Carolyn, Tom, Jillian, Mary, and the entire Zondervan team as well as David, Lowell, and Lis at CAA. Thank you for believing in me and allowing me to publish my first book! Love you guys so much.